REIGNITE

REIGNITE

TRANSFORM FROM **BURNED OUT**
TO **ON FIRE** AND FIND **NEW MEANING**
IN **YOUR CAREER** AND **LIFE**

Rekindle Your life with
Power, Passion, and Purpose

CLARK GAITHER, MD

NEW YORK

LONDON • NASHVILLE • MELBOURNE • VANCOUVER

REIGNITE

TRANSFORM FROM **BURNED OUT** TO **ON FIRE** AND FIND **NEW MEANING** IN **YOUR CAREER** AND **LIFE**

Published in New York, New York, by Morgan James Publishing. Morgan James is a trademark of Morgan James, LLC. www.MorganJamesPublishing.com

Proudly distributed by Publishers Group West®

Morgan James BOGO™

A **FREE** ebook edition is available for you or a friend with the purchase of this print book.

[   ]

CLEARLY SIGN YOUR NAME ABOVE

Instructions to claim your free ebook edition:
1. Visit MorganJamesBOGO.com
2. Sign your name CLEARLY in the space above
3. Complete the form and submit a photo of this entire page
4. You or your friend can download the ebook to your preferred device

ISBN 9781636981314 paperback
ISBN 9781636981321 ebook
Library of Congress Control Number:
2023930490

Interior Design by:
Chris Treccani
www.3dogcreative.net

Morgan James is a proud partner of Habitat for Humanity Peninsula and Greater Williamsburg. Partners in building since 2006.

Get involved today! Visit: www.morgan-james-publishing.com/giving-back

Gratefully,
To the organization and people that saved my life:
The North Carolina Physicians Health Program

TABLE OF CONTENTS

Foreword   xiii

Introduction   xv

On Fire to Burned Out: A Personal Story of Burnout   1

Burnout Is Different Than Stress   7

The Hallmarks of Job-Related Burnout   9
   Burning Out Is Different Than Smoldering Out   13

The High Costs of Burnout   15
   Employee Turnover   15
   Disruptive Behavior in the Workplace   16
   Burnout Costs on Multiple Levels   19

The Scope of Burnout   21

The Causes of Job-Related Burnout   25
   Individual Causes   25
   Organizational Causes   26
   Bottom Line   39

Your Preferred Future   41
    Taking Responsibility   42
    Do You Know What You Want?   44
    Eight Truths About Your Journey   46
    Ten Suggestions for Reality-Based Living   48
    The Barrier to Implementing New Ideas Isn't What You Think   51
    Seven Indicators of Lethal Complacency   52
    The Minimalist Guide to Indecision   55
    Do We Seize the Moment, or Does the Moment Seize Us?   56
    Success Rubs Off, But Only Onto Those in the Nearby Vicinity   58
    Sometimes You Just Have to Hit RESTART   60
    Don't Wait for Just the Right Time   62
    Is Your Future the Biggest Gamble of All?   64
    Why Chance Is Not an Option When It Comes to
    Your Preferred Future   66

Individual Remedies for Job-Related Burnout   69
    The REIGNITE Framework   69
    Resilience—Hardiness—Wellness   135
    When Resilience Really Counts   135
    Ten Steps Promoting Resilience You Absolutely Must Learn   137
    Eight Ways to Build or Strengthen Resilience   139

Work-Life Balance   143

Your Four Life Realms   145

Ten Reasons Why Only 2% Will Transform   145

Organizational Remedies for JRB   149
    The Cure   150
    The Bottom Line   151
    What to Expect from a Consultant   152

The Other Option: Self-Employment—Entrepreneurship 155

Engagement—the Polar Opposite of Burnout 157
    VIGOR 158
    DEDICATION 160
    ABSORPTION 162
    Remembering the Six Pathways to Engagement 164

From Burned Out to ON FIRE 167
    Happiness In the Pursuit of Dissatisfaction 167
    Successfully Avoiding Burnout (Slow and Steady!) 169

It's All Up to YOU! 173

REIGNITE Framework at a Glance 177

REFERENCES 179

FOREWORD

Working with impaired physicians is hard. Working with impaired and burned-out physicians is even harder. And yet, since Dr. Clark Gaither joined my team, I find that even the most difficult of cases can become easier.

As CEO of the North Carolina Physicians Health Program, my job allows me to be around some very intelligent people with some very difficult problems. The upside is that my job is very seldom boring; the downside is that my job is seldom boring. And frankly, the medical world we live in has been a taxing one; until about a year and a half ago, I wondered how we were going to make it. That all started to change when I hired Clark Gaither to be our medical director. Having Clark on our team has reinvigorated our organization and helped us to move out of what I believe was the spiral of organizational burnout.

You see, that is what is so special about Clark. I like to call him "Dr. Possible"; he can look at just about any situation and rather than giving in to the negativity, he can find a way to see the way through to a solution. His infectious laugh and genuine good nature make him able to disarm and engage others in a thoughtful dialogue about solutions rather than problems, and at some point in any conversation about a challenging situation, I see his eyes begin to gleam with possibilities. That is when I begin to relax and know that my team has a leader for any situation.

His command of the problem of burnout in our culture is both scary and encouraging. Scary because he has educated all of us to just how pervasive the issue of burnout is in our culture, and the numbers are truly frightening. Roughly 55 percent of physicians are experiencing some symptoms of burnout; trust me when I say this is a significant, underestimated problem, as that number is based on self-reporting. Encouraging; well, that is because as I referenced earlier, Clark is one of those people that helps others find the possible, the solution they didn't know was there, the way to weather a storm no matter what the situation. As we work at NCPHP to find ways to combat an epidemic of burnout in medical professionals, I feel incredibly lucky to have an expert like Clark to help us find out what possibilities exist for moving from a place of darkness to one of hope and light.

Enjoy this book. Take out your highlighter and your notepad, and make notes. Use the wisdom herein, and as I have, find out what it will take to go from "burned out" to "on fire" in your business, your career, and your life. And then, pass it along to someone you know that needs to find out what Dr. Possible can do for them.

Joseph P. Jordan, PhD
CEO of the North Carolina Physicians Health Program

INTRODUCTION

A t one time many years ago, my life had become completely unmanageable. I became an alcoholic, put my career as a family physician in jeopardy, and came ruinously close to losing everything for which I had worked so hard.

I was able to get sober and have been in continuous sobriety since January 23, 1990. Little did I realize that this was just the beginning of a lifelong transformation. There was much more in the way of personal disappointment and turmoil on the horizon, though I was unable to see it at the time and I was wholly unprepared for it when it arrived.

All of the years I have spent in the practice of medicine have not been great years. Yes, medicine has been good to me, and I believe I have been good at the practice of medicine. Yet, I have always felt as though something was missing. Have you ever felt this way at your job?

Added to that, after years of dedicated service to my patients and my community I developed a deepening dissatisfaction with my job. I came to feel emotionally drained most of the time. I seemed to be irritated by everything and everyone. I couldn't wait to get off work and lived for the weekends. At the same time, I began to dread going back into the office on Monday mornings.

Ever-increasing patient care mandates, unreasonable care guidelines, rule changes from government agencies and insurers, rapidly increasing costs, malpractice concerns, loss of autonomy when making decisions on behalf of my patients, time constraints during patient encounters, having to manage an increasing number of disease states with increasing severity among a rapidly growing and aging patient population, unreasonable and burdensome continuing medical education requirements—all of these things contributed to my unrest and dissatisfaction.

I felt used up. I was becoming very cynical. I was irritable and unhappy. I felt put upon by everyone and everything. I hadn't felt any joy or pleasure in my work for a very long time. Have you ever felt this way?

These feelings were spilling over into my personal life. It was only my 17th year in private practice, and I was a long way from retirement, but I knew, I *knew* something was wrong and something had to change. The dark mood I was in at work began to follow me home.

It took a few more years in private practice, further deterioration emotionally and physically, and a failed marriage for me to realize that for true happiness and fulfillment I would have to completely transform my life, my mindset. Transformation came by first increasing my self-awareness, and then by living a more authentic life, one more closely aligned with my core values. This transformation has brought me to the present. I have begun to share my experience, strength, and hope with others who feel as I once felt—burned out at work, in life, on living. My transformation has been nothing short of miraculous.

Not only do I believe every human being has the ability to change, I believe everyone has the ability to completely TRANSFORM their life using their own unique natural set of talents and abilities in close alignment with their core values. That is, if they so choose.

Everyone has the capacity to transform, to undergo a metamorphosis of the mind, body, and spirit in order to dream, design, and construct their own preferred future. I earnestly desire this for you, dear reader. I want you to come to know what I know. If you are suffering from the symptoms of burnout, it doesn't have to be that way.

Just know this upfront. If you want some things to change, you are going to have to change some things.

This book will show you how.

A Personal Story of Burnout

One day in 2009, I was at the office, immersed in the daily routine. Well, "the daily grind" is probably a more apt description of my routine at the time. I had just finished a rather difficult patient encounter. The patient, who was scheduled for a follow-up appointment and had a complicated medical history, limited resources, and little motivation to change, presented me with an extensive list of new complaints. I had less than ten minutes to deal with all of it, not an unusual occurrence.

The problems were difficult and disparate. The encounter ran long, about thirty-five minutes, and still I felt there were loose ends and more to be done, but other patients were waiting. I knew not all of them would be understanding of the long delay.

I was feeling mentally and emotionally exhausted. As I exited the room and looked up, there were four employees standing in line in the hallway, all waiting to ask me a question. Every exam room was full. As the first employee began to ask me a question, the phone rang at my desk nearby. On the way to answer the phone, my pager went off. Even before I picked up the phone, I heard a clear and loud voice inside my head screaming, "I can't do this anymore."

At that moment, something inside of me shifted. Well, it actually snapped, but shifted sounds better. In that instant I knew something had to change. I felt nothing inside but desperation. The feeling had been budding, brewing, building inside of me for some time.

I very much enjoyed my work when I first began my medical career. I was very thankful for having such a great job, which combined my love of science, problem solving, and an abiding sense of curiosity. I got to help people feel better and live longer lives. I mean, how great is that?!

Even so, I always felt as though something was missing, like I had stepped into a role which did not completely suit me, feeling as though the profession didn't fit me just right or that I didn't fit the profession just right.

Have you ever felt this way?

The best way I can explain what this felt like to me is by way of an example. As you know, what physicians do day-in and day-out requires the use of a lot of exam gloves. Over the years, I have tried on a myriad of gloves in various sizes from an array of manufacturers, composed of various materials such as latex, PVC, nitrile, synthetic rubber, etc. I've tried them all, whole sizes and half sizes.

None of them ever felt as though they fit my hands just right, not perfectly. I wore them, and I could always get the job done while wearing them, but this "not quite right" feeling was emblematic of how I felt throughout my career in medicine.

I was never able to shake that feeling. In spite of feeling this way, I put my head down and worked hard for many years. I was able to accomplish a lot and succeed in many areas of medicine as a clinician, speaker, volunteer, and teacher. The price for this was high. I was building hurdles rather than clearing them.

In his book *The Big Leap*, Gay Hendricks talks about operating in your zone of excellence versus your zone of genius. He points out how you can be extremely competent and successful in a given area yet still miss or fall short of your zone of genius based on the choices you make. Medicine was my zone of excellence, not my zone of genius.

Even after I was fortunate enough to be named Family Physician of The Year in 2002 by the North Carolina Academy of Family Physicians and become a Fellow of the American Academy of Family Physicians in 2010, the feeling never changed. All the while I felt meant for some other purpose. Over many years, this feeling began to affect my practice.

The truth is, I overextended myself in trying to be the "everything to everybody" doctor. I was trying to do too much for everyone around me and not enough for myself. I was a people pleaser, and I definitely had a hard time saying no to anyone. Can you identify with some of this?

On that fateful day in 2009, I went to my practice partner and shared with him I either had to make some changes or I was going to have to quit practicing medicine. I told him exactly how I felt—angry, overworked, dissatisfied, and unappreciated. I had come to feel I was no longer making a difference in the lives of my patients. It wasn't true, but it was how I felt.

I didn't blame him in any way, but I secretly resented him in a way because he didn't seem to feel any of what I was feeling. He is a great doctor and friend. His life seemed happy and balanced. I didn't know what was wrong with me, why I felt as I did. I just knew something had to change.

I had read a few articles on the subject of physician burnout, so I went to the internet for more information. Once I read the symptoms, I quickly became convinced I aptly fit the description, well, just like a hand fits a glove. I was burned out!

So, I put an action plan together for myself and began taking some steps to fix what was broken.

The first thing I did was go to a three-day work week in the office. I made each of those days an hour longer, but now I was off from work four days out of seven. I took a cut in salary, but I would have worked for free just to feel better and to have a shot at happiness and fulfillment in my work. I began to use the extra time to get my mental, emotional, physical, and spiritual houses in order.

I resigned from over half a dozen boards, staying only on one about which I was most passionate to serve. I read, traveled, ran, and rekindled old interests outside of medicine for which I had previously made no time.

I wondered if my colleagues and other professionals were suffering from burnout. It didn't take but a few minutes and a Google search to see this was a huge problem.

I began to study job-related burnout in depth, its warning signs, symptoms, consequences, and treatment. I gave talks on the subject, and they were well received. I found many colleagues who identified precisely with the way I was feeling. Although burnout rates are screamingly high and climbing among healthcare providers, there are detectable burnout rates in every profession, in relationships, even in life and living.

The steps I took and others made all the difference. I began to enjoy the practice of medicine again. I developed a new patience for my patients. Energy returned. I felt more at peace. I became hopeful for the future once more and began to achieve a more balanced life.

Ask yourself the following:

- Do you feel that you are merely existing rather than living, laboring at a job that you detest where your true passions cannot be expressed or where your talents cannot be developed or constructively explored?
- Do you feel that you have somehow sidestepped your life's calling, that something profound is missing, that your life or your job is like a pair of gloves that have never felt as though they fit you quite right?
- Do you feel that you have not fully developed your natural talents and abilities, have no opportunity to use them, or believe you have no natural talents or abilities?
- Do you feel burned out on life or on living, that there is no fire, drive, passion, or sense of purpose deep inside of you?

Just know it doesn't have to be this way. My primary focus and the purpose of this book are to help you identify and erase the causes and destructive effects of burnout and to assist you in transforming your life by:

- Increasing self-awareness by identifying your top ten core values and your #1 core value.
- Identifying and developing your true inner passions.
- Identifying, developing, and employing your natural talents and abilities for purposeful work.
- Finding joy, happiness, and fulfillment through purposeful work.
- Positively remodeling your mindset and fine-tuning it for a lifetime of success.
- Assessing the health and needs of all four of your personal realms—the mental, emotional, physical, and spiritual realms.
- Unleashing your creative potential.

Have these goals in mind as you proceed through this book. All of them are imminently attainable with guidance and the proper tools.

BURNOUT IS DIFFERENT THAN STRESS

At some point in your career, have you ever said to yourself, "I'm burned out"? Sure, any job can lead to frustration from time to time, which can cause temporary negative feelings about one's work. Negative feelings that persist and get worse with time, though, can actually lead to something called job-related burnout. But what does it really mean to be burned out?

Most of the time, the symptoms of job-related burnout (JRB), or burnout of any sort, are incorrectly assigned to stress. Burnout is quite different from stress, though. You can be stressed without being burned out, but if you are burned out, I can say with 100 percent assurance you are stressed. As you will see, stress does not cause burnout, but burnout can cause stress.

Treating burnout as stress is not only the wrong thing to do, but is 180 degrees the exact opposite of the right thing to do. Stress-reduction strategies might help in the short term, but not in the long run. Any positive benefits from stress reduction, such as yoga, meditation, stress management, or mindfulness training will be temporary at best.

You can take a dedicated, on-fire, energetic, passionate, and purpose-driven person and place them in the wrong work environment, or a toxic work environment, and you will burn them out. Stress-reduction strategies may offer some relief, but if you put the same individual back into the same work environment, their symptoms will return because the underlying causes have not been properly addressed. This will needlessly delay proper management.

Here are the primary differences between burnout and stress:

Stress	Job-related Burnout
Characterized by over-engagement.	Characterized by disengagement.
Emotions are overactive.	Emotions are blunted.
Produces urgency and hyperactivity.	Produces helplessness and hopelessness.
Leads to loss of energy.	Leads to loss of ideals, motivation, and hope.
Leads to anxiety disorders.	Leads to detachment and depression.
With stress, the damage is primarily physical.	With burnout, the damage is primarily emotional.
Prolonged and excessive stress may kill you prematurely (cardiovascular disease or suppression of the immune system).	Burnout will make your life not seem worth living and increases your risk of suicide.
Stress is more easily identified and treated.	Burnout can be much more difficult to manage.
Stress is almost always recognized by the individual.	Burnout may not be recognized as such by the individual; symptoms will likely be attributed to some other cause.

Looking at these differences, it is readily apparent that the approach to the identification, mitigation, elimination, and prevention of stress versus burnout should be quite different.

Let's next take a close look at the hallmarks of job-related burnout.

THE HALLMARKS OF JOB-RELATED BURNOUT

The discipline of medicine is inherently difficult. There is a lot to know. Skill is required. The responsibilities are great. The ability to engender trust, demonstrate competency, and exude compassion is an absolute necessity. An enormous amount of mental, emotional, physical, and spiritual energy is required for the job. All of this, and more, is needed to become "the good doctor."

In my profession, medicine, burnout rates are among the highest. Naturally, you would want or expect a physician to be on fire with passion and purpose for the practice of medicine, right? Especially if that person were *your* doctor. Tragically, this is not the case for the majority of physicians currently practicing within the US.

The house of medicine is on fire, not with passion-driven purpose, but with a majority of doctors who are burning out. The flames of passion for our profession have been replaced by the all-consuming fires of job-related burnout. We are in the midst of a national medical emergency with physicians burning out.

What once began in slow motion is now rapidly accelerating. A recent study published by Shanafelt et al in the December 2015 issue of *Mayo Clinic Proceedings* documented a rise to 54.4% from 45.5% in the number of physicians reporting at least one hallmark of burnout (out of three) in the span of just three years, from 2011 to 2014. Today, six out of ten physicians would quit medicine, right now, if they were financially able to do so.

I know firsthand how it feels to be burned out. It is a miserable feeling, almost one of complete helplessness and hopelessness. I had hit all three hallmarks of burnout.

The hallmarks of job-related burnout were succinctly described by Dr. Christina Maslach in 1981. She and her associate developed the Maslach Burnout Inventory (MBI), which is still used as the industry gold standard for measuring burnout rates. A twenty-two item questionnaire using a seven-point scale for responses ("Never to Every Day"), the MBI yields consistent results with sensitivity (true positive rate) and specificity (true negative rate).

The three principal hallmarks of job-related burnout are: emotional exhaustion, depersonalization, and a lack of a sense of personal accomplishment. Let's take a look at them one-by-one.

- Emotional Exhaustion—A feeling of being emotionally depleted to the point where you feel you can no longer give of yourself, at an emotional or psychological level, to your company or the people you serve. You feel you have nothing left to give. KEYWORD: Exhaustion

- Depersonalization—The development of negative and cynical feelings leading to a callous and dehumanized perception of patients, clients, or customers, which further leads to detachment and to the view that they   are somehow deserving of their problems and troubles. KEYWORD: Cynicism

- Lack of a Sense of Personal Accomplishment—You feel so little reward from what you do that there is a tendency to evaluate yourself in negative terms, which leads to dissatisfaction and unhappiness in your work, creating a lack of a sense of personal accomplishment. In short, you feel that what you do no longer makes a difference. KEYWORD: Inefficacy

Men and women will register these slightly differently. Women will usually proceed through the three of these in the order presented. Men will usually become cynical first, followed by emotional exhaustion. Men may or may not hit the third hallmark of a lack of a sense of personal accomplishment. Most men will always feel their work has some meaning, at least to them.

These hallmarks are the symptoms of burnout, not the underlying causes, which I will cover in another chapter. In varying degree, some combination of these hallmarks will always be present when someone is burned out at work, in a relationship, at home, or even on living.

One thing is certain: if an individual can identify the presence of these hallmarks, they are either burning out or burned out. As you will see, the costs of job-related burnout are devastatingly high, not only for the individual employee but the organizations they work for as a whole.

Individuals who become burned out are at risk for chronic unhappiness, increased irritability, depression, anxiety, mood swings, suicidal thoughts, suicidal actions, alcoholism, and drug abuse. Besides the obvious consequences of these, there is also a potential for a great loss of knowledge, expertise, and innovation to a company, organization, or society at large.

Tragically, a person's creativity can become stymied or destroyed by burnout, and someone's passion and sense of purpose may be completely subverted.

In her book *The Truth About Burnout*, Dr. Christina Maslach observes, "What started out as important, meaningful, fascinating work becomes unpleasant, unfulfilling, and meaningless." She further adds, "The positive feelings of enthusiasm, dedication, security, and enjoyment fade away and are replaced by anger, anxiety and depression."

How can you determine if you or someone you care about is burned out or burning out? Listen for these statements of warning.

- I feel used up, empty, or dead inside.
- I feel hopeless, helpless, or lost.
- I feel I have nothing left to give.
- I go to work, and all I feel is frustration.
- I have lost enthusiasm for the work I used to love.
- I feel trapped, overwhelmed, overloaded, or overworked.
- If, "I love my job," has been replaced by, "I hate my job!"

The individual experiencing burnout may view this as some sort of personal crisis of their own making, and in some circumstances, it is. But, burnout more than likely represents a dysfunctional work environment. Either way, there is much that can be done to alleviate and prevent burnout.

There are steps that can be taken to introduce or restore an individual to a state of engagement, the opposite of burnout, which I will cover in a later chapter.

If you are burned out in your job, there are warning signs and symptoms everyone should know. If you don't know the symptoms of burnout, you may mistake them for something else. This can lead to a delay in addressing the underlying issues and needlessly prolong your suffering.

People who are burned out rarely recognize it as such. They may incorrectly ascribe their feelings to being ambivalent, anxious, stressed, depressed, sad, or irritable. Although burnout can lead to all of these mood changes, they are not the underlying cause. They are just symptoms.

Those around someone who is burned out may be left to wonder if the change in their behavior is due to stress, depression, drug use, relationship problems, money problems, or personality/ character defects. Again, burnout is not usually suspected as the cause.

How can you tell if you are burned out or burning out? Your inner mood or feelings associated with job-related burnout can include:

- Feeling more and more time-pressured at work.
- A sense of dread associated with going to work.
- A sense of relief that the weekend has finally arrived.
- A lack of recognition or not feeling rewarded for good work.
- Feeling that job demands are unclear or unreasonable.
- Either work is no longer challenging or it has become overwhelmingly challenging.
- Work seems chaotic or too high-pressure.
- A sense there is no time you can take off from work without consequences.
- Feeling that you have to be too many things to far too many people.

- Feeling as though you have no help.
- Feeling as though you no longer make a difference.
- Difficulty or inability to concentrate.
- You lack close and supportive relationships in both your work and personal life.
- Less patience. Less empathy. Less enthusiasm.
- More irritable. More intolerant. More exhausted. More cynical.
- Feeling disengaged, unmotivated, uninterested, or uninteresting.
- Feeling as though life is no longer worth living.
- A feeling you should be doing something else.
- A feeling you do not fit in your profession, or it does not fit you.
- Feeling as though you have nothing left to give.
- Continuously questioning yourself: "Is this all there is to life? Is there nothing more?"

Of course, there are other feelings, but these are the ones most often identified in people suffering from burnout. The great news about burnout is its 100 percent reversible, treatable, and preventable. When I realized I was suffering from job burnout, I made some very simple changes right away, which made all the difference in the way I felt toward myself, my patients, and my profession.

The key is recognizing the signs and symptoms of burnout and how it differs from job stress. Once burnout is recognized, steps can be taken to ameliorate or eliminate the job-employee mismatches that lead to job-related burnout.

Burning Out Is Different Than Smoldering Out

I have seen individuals who have become apathetic about their passion in life but who are not yet burned out. I coined the phrase, "smoldering out," to describe symptoms much less severe than burnout.

Smoldering out can best be described as a loss of enthusiasm and energy for one's passion without feeling emotionally exhausted, cynical, or inefficacious. Smoldering out does not include the symptoms of burnout. It is temporary, can occur at any time, and is more easily eliminated or prevented.

Although it is decidedly different than burnout, anyone who suffers from burnout will always feel smoldered out. However, you can be smoldered out without being burned out. Here are some of the causes of smoldering out and some steps you can take to reignite your passion.

1. Work has become too routine—Routine can lead to boredom after a while. If your passion has become too routine, then you may have put your creativity on the shelf. It may be time to dust it off and unleash your creative self again. Creativity and excitement dance hand in hand. If you are continuously creating something new and different, then you are probably still very excited, even emotional, when it comes to your passion.

2. You are sidetracked and drifting—Perhaps you have let yourself drift away from your intended purpose in life. You may have lost your passionate drive because you have pivoted or turned into a headwind or in the wrong direction. Shut down the interference. Eliminate your distractions. Redirect, recalibrate, and refocus yourself on what you were meant to do and be.

3. You are trying to do too much for too many—When you found work for which you were passionate, work then became play for you, and you were happy. Then, everyone wanted what you were selling. Now, it just seems like work again. You began to work harder, trying to produce more and more. But now you feel overextended. Or maybe you are over-promising, outstripping your ability to produce comfortably and in a way that suits you and your craft or art. When you suffer, your work will suffer. Maybe it is time to slow down and savor your gifts and talents. It is probably better for your product to be essential and relatively scarce versus pedestrian and in relative abundance.

In the next chapter, we will look at the high costs associated with burnout.

THE HIGH COSTS OF BURNOUT

The keyword hallmarks of burnout are exhaustion, cynicism, and inefficacy. In short, with burnout you can end up an exhausted, ineffective cynic. I don't know about you, but that doesn't sound good to me.

I have described the differences between burnout and stress. Burnout represents more to the individual than just job-related stress. Burnout is a much more serious state that requires more immediate and drastic intervention because the symptoms and consequences can be profound. Burnout is a condition that can leave an individual feeling helpless, hopeless, confused, isolated, and lost.

Individuals who become burned out are at risk for poor job performance, chronic unhappiness, increased irritability, depression, anxiety, and mood swings. Even suicidal thoughts, suicidal actions, alcoholism, and drug abuse are documented consequences of burnout. Bottom line: if you are burned out, you will never feel you are living a life of purpose with passion.

Employee Turnover

Not only is burnout bad for the employee; a business with burned-out employees suffers as well.

All companies and organizations want to attract and retain top business talent. This is a given if you want to run a successful business. It would be counterproductive to build the best workforce one could hope for, only to lose way too many valuable employees to rapid turnover. Employee recruitment, installation, and training mean big expenditures and a huge drag on the bottom line.

One of the biggest preventable causes of high employee turnover is job-related burnout. It is a little understood fact that most employees do not burn themselves out. A full 90 percent of the time it is the work environment that burns out the employee.

You can take a dedicated, on-fire employee who functions efficiently with enthusiasm and impassioned purpose, put them in the wrong work environment, and you will burn them out most every time. This can be mitigated when present and prevented when absent.

Why is this important? Burned-out employees create workplace problems, which demand resources. Dissatisfied workers lead to inferior products and services, which leads to dissatisfied patients, clients, or customers. Dissatisfied consumers lead to a loss of business and falling profit margins.

Disruptive Behavior in the Workplace

One of the worst consequences of workplace burnout, and one of the most difficult to deal with, is an employee who is acting out with disruptive behavior.

If you work in any organization long enough, you will run into someone exhibiting disruptive behavior. I can speak firsthand for the profession of medicine. Estimates suggest that just three to five percent of physicians are responsible for most of the disruptive behavior in medicine. But you can find disruptive behavior in any organization.

While 3–5% doesn't sound like much, a disruptive employee can wreak havoc among the other employees. Following *Pareto's Principle* (a theory that roughly 80% of the outcomes of a given situation come from 20% of the causes), 80 percent of the problems an organization may face can come from a few individuals displaying disruptive behavior.

Disruptive behavior can have negative effects on patients, clients, or customers. Within an organization, such behavior can be a steady drain on morale, thereby decreasing productivity and leading to high staff turn-over, which can further degrade work quality.

Even if you work within an organization replete with competent and engaged employees, a disruptive employee can create an environment conducive to employee burnout.

At the extreme, disruptive behavior can undermine safety, create hostile work environments, and even generate dangerous work-related inter-actions and encounters.

There is often a reluctance to deal with disruptive behavior. There is always the hope that the individual will one day just stop their bad and intolerable behavior. This strategy falls into the category of watching the paint dry. Unfortunately, disruptive individuals never see the light until they feel some heat.

Other reasons for a reluctance to confront individuals displaying dis-ruptive behavior include financial motives, threat of litigation or other forms of retribution, or even fear of violence. Studies have demonstrated very clearly the costs of allowing disruptive behavior to continue are far higher.

Due to the high costs of disruptive behavior, it is very important to rec-ognize the associated behavior patterns and give prompt attention to the individual(s) involved. Here are some examples of disruptive behavior:

- Cursing, profane or disrespectful language
- Yelling, screaming, or shouting in anger
- Berating, belittling, or insulting others
- Sexual advances, comments, or innuendo
- Intimidation, sarcasm, and stinging criticism
- Nonverbal lewd gestures
- Passive-aggressive or vindictive behavior
- Throwing of objects and/or slamming doors
- Bullying, intimidating, or demeaning conversations and commu-nications
- Criticizing other employees, staff, clients, employer, or other organizations in front of others

Disruptive behavior in individuals must be dealt with squarely and firmly. If the individual is an otherwise valued employee, then an intervention with subsequent behavioral modification training should be undertaken.

Of course, the best way to deal with disruptive behavior is to prevent such behavior in the first place. This can be easily accomplished by putting systems in place to effectively deal with aberrant workplace behavior. The following components might be included:

- The establishment of a code of conduct
- Creating a reporting and monitoring system for disruptive behavior
- Training and educating employees on disruptive behavior
- Establishing a resolution algorithm for handling an employee exhibiting disruptive behavior

An organization-wide policy with uniform enforcement relating to disruptive behavior can make for a much more pleasant, safe, and effective environment in which to work. This easily translates into the production of a higher quality product or service.

If you have been the recipient of disruptive behavior in the workplace, you might try some of these steps aimed at alleviating or eliminating the behavior:

- First, try speaking directly with the individual about their behavior, but only if you feel it is safe to do so and there is a chance they might respond favorably.
- If you feel it is unsafe to speak with them directly, or if you do and the individual responds unfavorably and your anonymity can be protected, you have a duty to report the behavior and the individual involved.
- Seek advice from within your company's Employee Assistance Program (EAP) if there is one available, or from the personnel manager.
- If all else fails and the disruptive behavior is not properly addressed and the work environment becomes harmfully toxic, don't just

stand and take it. Start looking elsewhere for a better place of employment, one which safeguards valued employees from this kind of harm.

Have you ever noticed disruptive behavior in your past or present work environments? If so, what was the outcome? How did it affect your work or the work of those around you?

Burnout Costs on Multiple Levels

Businesses can be destroyed by workplace burnout. It is amazing how many times this scenario is repeated every year in businesses all across this country. It just doesn't have to be this way.

Here is the bottom line for organizations. Failure to address burnout in the workplace can result in a dysfunctional workforce, high staff turnover, and inferior products or services. The result is a type of internal rot, not to mention the financial devastation this can bring.

Job-related burnout will increase an organization's direct and indirect costs and decrease profits by:

- Causing high rates of employee turnover
- Decreasing employee satisfaction
- Increasing employee absenteeism
- Increasing employee complaints
- Increasing customer complaints
- Decreasing the quality of products and services
- Creating hostile or toxic work environments
- Increasing lawsuits
- Decreasing consumer traffic/sales

In my profession, the direct costs associated with replacing just one physician can range from $150,000 to over $1,000,000, depending on the provider's specialty. Associated indirect costs will push this number even higher. It is the same for the CEOs of large companies and organizations.

For other professionals, such as teachers, firefighters, police officers, social workers, managerial and clerical staff, the direct costs for employee replacement ranges from one-and-a-half to three times their annual salaries.

Those who mind the bottom line should know that eliminating or preventing workplace job-related burnout isn't just cost effective; it is income generating by decreasing costs and increasing profits. If your goal is to get an administrator's attention to make some changes in the workplace to reduce or eliminate burnout, here is what you can tell them.

Eliminating or preventing burnout will:

- Decrease employee turnover and improve retention of needed talent
- Increase employee satisfaction and decrease employee complaints
- Decrease employee absenteeism
- Improve customer satisfaction and decrease customer complaints
- Increase the quality of products and services
- Eliminate work hostility and promote workplace harmony
- Decrease the threat of lawsuits

Under this scenario, everyone wins. The amount of money spent to eliminate or prevent workplace burnout will be small compared to drain on the bottom line burnout will cause.

THE SCOPE OF BURNOUT

Any profession you can name has a detectable rate of burnout. Some are worse than others, and some professions have lower burnout rates. This begs the question: is it the local work environment or the inherent nature of a job that causes or determines the rate of burnout?

Not a lot of solid data is published on burnout rates among the many different professions, so more studies are needed. You can look at job turnover rates or reported stress levels, but these are not the same as the job burnout rate, which has a specific set of causes. Some professions are heavy on the entry level end of the spectrum, and this can skew turnover rates. Also, I've already discussed how stress and burnout are decidedly different.

Where turnover rates and stress levels are simultaneously elevated, you can bet burnout rates will be high, even though the exact rate will remain unknown unless precisely measured with a good instrument such as the MBI.

From the Bureau of Labor and Statistics we get the following data for 2016. The jobs with the highest turnover rates are:

- Retail: 67%
- Food Service: 62.6%
- Information Technology: > 50%
- Nursing: 43%
- Child Care: > 30%

- Hospitality: 31:34%
- Sales: > 66%

According to research by *Business News Daily*, the ten most and least stressful jobs of 2016 are (descending order):

LEAST Stressful	MOST Stressful
#10. Forklift Operator	#10. Taxi Driver
#9. Librarian	#9. Newspaper Reporter
#8. Dietician	#8. Broadcaster
#7. Seamstress/Tailor	#7. Senior Corporate Exec.
#6. Medical Laboratory Technician	#6. Public Relations Exec
#5. Jeweler	#5. Event Coordinator
#4. Medical Records Technician	#4. Police Officer
#3. University Professor (tenured)	#3. Airline Pilot
#2. Audiologist	#2. Firefighter
#1. Hair Stylist	#1. Enlisted Military Personnel

Although careers in my profession, healthcare, didn't make the top ten list of the most stressful jobs, it is an industry for which we have actual rates for burnout that have been scientifically measured. These statistics create another striking contrast between actual burnout rates versus on-the-job stress or job turnover rates.

Take a look at these awful burnout statistics from the field of medicine:

- In 1987, an AMA survey showed that 44% of physician respondents over the age of forty would not choose medicine as a career if they had it to do all over again.
- A 2001 survey of physicians in Massachusetts found 62.3% dissatisfied with their practice environment.

- A survey by the Kaiser Family Foundation in 2002 revealed that 45% of physicians would not recommend that a young person choose medicine as a career choice.
- A 2007 survey of primary care physicians found 38.7% were somewhat or very dissatisfied with the practice of medicine.
- A 2011 survey of 2,069 physicians by VITAL WorkLife and Cejka Search, a Minneapolis-based company, found 87% of respondents felt moderately or severely stressed or burned out daily. The median age was 45 with an average of 13 years in practice.
- In a survey that was presented to 13,000 physicians in 2012, six out of ten physicians would quit today if financially able to do so. That's 60%!
- A 2012 study of 7,288 physicians published in the Archives of Internal Medicine revealed that 46% reported at least one symptom of burnout.
- From an Academic Medicine paper dated July 2012, 14% of respondents had seriously considered leaving their own institution during the prior year and 21% had seriously considered leaving academic medicine altogether due to dissatisfaction.
- Burnout rates exceeded 70% in Radiology. Other specialties with higher-than-average rates of burnout are Emergency Medicine, Family Medicine, General Internal Medicine, and Neurology.
- One report shows that nearly 60% of practicing radiologists surveyed had at least one symptom of burnout.
- The burnout rate among female physicians at 60% is higher than the male physician burnout rate of 52%.
- Burnout rates are highest in the 46 to 55 and over 66 age brackets.
- Using the Primary Care Evaluation of Mental Disorders screening instrument, the percentage of physicians who may have been depressed was 37.8%, much higher than the national average across the general population.
- Suicide rates among physicians are higher than rates in the general population, 1.41 times higher for men and 2.27 times higher for

women. Over 400 physicians committed suicide in 2016. Having a job problem that contributed to suicide was highly predictive that the job was that of a physician.

• A recent study in Mayo Clinic Proceedings documented a rise to 54.4% from 45.5% in the number of physicians reporting at least one of the hallmarks (1 of 3) of burnout in the span of just three years, from 2011 to 2014.

So it goes: on and on and on. As you can see by the timelines above, burnout rates in healthcare are not only getting worse—they are accelerating. Other professions within medicine are similarly affected, such as nurses, medical coders, physician assistants, family nurse practitioners, and others. Burnout rates are almost as catastrophically high among social workers, teachers, police officers, firefighters, and attorneys.

Another surrogate measure of job burnout is job satisfaction data. What does the national picture of job satisfaction look like? A November 2015 Gallup survey found 51% of employees sampled were considering looking for a new job. While this does not reflect an actual burnout rate of 51%, it is indicative of a lot of job dissatisfaction. At least some of this dissatisfaction has at its base job burnout.

The scope of burnout is both broad and deep and affects all professions to varying degrees. What is contributing to this? What are the causes? There are many factors, and all of them have at their roots six major job-employee mismatches that will lead to JRB. We will explore those in the next chapter.

THE CAUSES OF JOB-RELATED BURNOUT

According to Christina Maslach, author of *The Truth About Burnout*, there are two completely different approaches to dealing with JRB. Which approach you employ depends on the originating source of the burnout—an individual approach or an organizational approach. Individual approaches are used when individuals burn themselves out. This occurs only ten percent of the time. Organizational approaches are used when the work environment burns out the individual. A full ninety percent of the time, it is the work environment that burns out the employee.

Individual Causes

I can state with complete assurance: if an individual burns themself out, it's because their life is out of balance. A life out of balance is created when an improper level of attention is given to one of an individual's four life realms—the mental, emotional, physical, and spiritual realms. Either too much attention is given to one or two of the four realms, or too little attention is paid to a realm.

For harmonious living, these realms must be in relative balance with one another. It is impossible to live a life of happiness and passion-driven purpose if your life is out of balance.

Activities that contribute to a life out of balance include but aren't limited to:

- Workaholism
- Cessation of Lifetime Learning
- Emotional Immaturity
- Mood Disorders
- Drug Addiction/Alcoholism
- Disconnection from Nature/People
- Lack of Physical Exercise
- Overeating/Obesity
- Poor Work Ethic
- Narrow Interests
- Being Stuck

There are remedies for a life out of balance, which I will address in a section just up ahead.

Organizational Causes

The Six Major Job-Employee Mismatches of Burnout

The three principal hallmarks of job-related burnout—emotional exhaustion, depersonalization, and lack of a sense of personal accomplishment—are extremely good indicators of the presence of burnout. However, they are not the causes of job burnout. They are only the symptoms or results of burnout.

Certainly, a person could choose a profession to which they are not well suited. But more often than not, individuals can find themselves in a job where there is substantial conflict between the demands of the job and their core values. When this occurs, the potential for job burnout is high.

Ninety percent of the time it is not the employee who burns himself out; it is the work environment which burns out the employee.

There are six major mismatches between the job and employee that cause job-related burnout. A major mismatch is created any time there is sufficient conflict between the nature of the person and the nature of the job the person is being asked to do. Wherever these mismatches occur to a high degree, employees will be found who are either burned out or burning out. This has a tremendous negative impact on organizations and the employees within them.

If you are an employee, you don't want to risk burnout because it is complete misery. Burnout can cause you to hate your job, increase your absenteeism, decrease your performance, make you cynical, completely exhaust you, and even depress you. You will even make less money if you are working burned out because you will be less efficient and less productive with higher rates of absenteeism.

Unfortunately, when the symptoms of burnout are being displayed, rather than an organization attacking the underlying causes, the individual often becomes the sole focus of any effort to alleviate their symptoms. It surprises many to discover the underlying job / employee mismatches are not created by the individual employee. Ninety percent of the time they are caused by the work environment.

In their book, *The Truth About Burnout*, Christina Maslach and Michael P. Leiter explain the causes of burnout lie more in the job environment than within the individual. They have identified six major mismatches between people and their jobs which, when left unattended to properly, will lead to burnout. Every employer and every organization should be vigilant for these burnout inducing conditions.

#1. Work Overload

Downsizing, budget cuts, layoffs, and reorganization efforts usually result in three things: more work intensity, more demands on time, and more job complexity. In short, people are required to do ever more with less. This can leave individuals feeling exhausted emotionally, mentally, and physically.

Businesses are in business to make money. You cannot stay in business otherwise. When costs are rising ahead of profits and product prices are raised to what markets will bear, then the only other way to maintain profits is to institute cost-cutting measures. Unless you are in business solo, employee salaries are the largest business expenditure you will have. If you are the owner of a business with shrinking profit margins, then letting any superfluous employees go is the easiest and fastest first step back toward profitability. That is the employer's perspective.

However, once you have removed any non-essential employees, further reductions in staffing will begin to impact the functions of all remaining employees. With fewer and fewer hands to do the work, work intensity and complexity must increase within ever smaller per-task time frames. That is the employee's perspective.

Eventually, a point is reached when the demands of the job outstrip and outpace the ability of the individual to adequately perform the job. The employee suffers, the product or service suffers, the business suffers, and ultimately the customer suffers.

I hear employees talk badly about bosses who continue to pile work on their desks or ask them to take on and manage new responsibilities. In my profession, doctors are asked to see more and more patients. The employee, of course, feels obligated to try and do the extra work.

Employees are often loath or fearful to say to their manager or boss, "No more. I can't possibly do all of this work." Or, "I have all I can manage at this time," and refuse any requests to the contrary. The managers or bosses, never hearing an emphatic protest, continue to ask the employees to bear ever more of the workload. Even when protests are made or complaints are lodged, many bosses may dismiss them with statements like: "Oh, I'm sure you will manage," or "This is just temporary until things improve," or, worse, "If you can't do the work, I'm sure someone else can or will."

Both bosses and employees will often buy into the hopeful notion of multitasking. I hear the word multitasking, and I just laugh. Of all the silly notions to come down the pike in the last 20 years, this has to be among the worst and most absurd.

Multitasking is a myth. The human brain can do one thing at a time very well or multiple functions at a time poorly. There is no such thing as multitasking if you have a requirement for excellence. Business and manufacturing operations have become so complex that multitasking has become an impossibility. If you ever doubt this, have a conversation with someone touting the benefits of multitasking and ask if they would be in favor of having a surgeon multitasking while performing a life-saving operation on one of their family members or on themselves. No? Well, maybe they would love the concept of a multitasking airline pilot or air traffic controller.

But, with great and sometimes valiant efforts, the employee often does somehow manage the ever-increasing workloads, which only serves to reinforce the boss's notion that the employees can handle all the work they can dole out. This leaves the door open for future workload increases.

So begins a circular, downward spiral toward employee burnout and business failures. You know, it just doesn't have to be this way. There is a way out of this work-overload, burnout trap, which I will cover later.

#2. Lack of Control

For most people, flying on a commercial airliner is the quintessential experience of a complete lack of control. This is mentioned often when people are expressing their fears over flying. A complete lack of control in one's work is even worse, as it is a front-running cause of job burnout.

Have you ever been in a situation as a customer with a problem that had an obvious and easy solution but the person helping you couldn't help you because of a company policy or rule? Maybe both of you knew what had to be done and both of you felt the futile frustration of an inability to act quickly and responsibly.

Perhaps you were the employee who could not act on the customer's behalf or apply an obvious solution to a problem at work because of company rules. Lack of control is another of the six job-employee mismatches that can lead to burnout at work.

Unfortunately, most large companies and organizations throughout the country are trending toward centralized control, just like governmental policies. Cookie-cutter approaches to producing a product or providing a service are often employed in order to control costs and streamline operations. More times than not, though, the employee feels overly controlled and grows to resent or hate it.

Organizations that become intolerant of creative problem solving in lieu of centralized control squelch individual autonomy. This reduces an employee's capacity to set limits, exercise problem solving, select individualized approaches to work, allocate resources, and set priorities. The overall effect is a loss of interest in the job and monumental frustration.

In her book *The Truth About Burnout*, Dr. Christina Maslach asserts the following:

> *"People want the opportunity to make choices and decisions, use their ability to think and solve problems, and have some input in the process of achieving the outcome for which they will be held accountable. There is a world of difference between being accountable and being constrained by rigid policies and tight monitoring."*

Unfortunately, most large companies and organizations throughout the country today are trending toward centralized control. This is especially true in the healthcare arena. Cookie-cutter approaches to producing a product or providing a service, as in treating patients, are often employed in order to control costs. More times than not, it is the employee who gets overly controlled. Centralized control seeks to take the responsibility for decision-making away from the employee. The unintended consequence of this is an employee who no longer feels responsible for what transpires at work because, in essence, the employee no longer is responsible.

Under these circumstances, employees no longer feel empowered to improve conditions on the job. Innovation goes out the window. With more and more centralized control, they get the unintended messages of: "You're too stupid," "You have poor judgment," "We can't trust you," "You're inept," and, "You're not capable."

Unable to act promptly, decisively, and responsibly, an employee may become the object of ridicule and anger from other members of the team or from customers. Cold and automated management becomes cold and automated work staff performance. The overall effect is a loss of interest in the job and monumental frustration and anger—the emotional hallmarks of job-related burnout as identified by Dr. Maslach.

You know, it just doesn't have to be this way.

Alternatively, centralized control could mean allowing more individual employee autonomy within set guidelines rather than relying on strict and rigid rules for every decision to be made. The goal should be to foster individual creativity and innovation in decision making rather than squelching it.

#3. Insufficient Rewards

Market forces cause organizations to focus on reducing costs, which in turn reduces their capacity to reward their employees in meaningful ways. People seek tangible and intangible rewards from meaningful work, such as money, security, recognition, benefits, etc. Intrinsic rewards are also important to workers, such as feeling satisfied with one's work, a feeling that a contribution is being made, or a sense that opportunities are available for growth or to be innovative and creative.

Whether you are talking about tangible or intangible rewards, people must derive one, the other, or both from the work they do.

Where there is little reward, expect little effort and poor results. If rewards are lacking, people naturally begin to wonder why they are working so hard.

This is a very simple equation, no factoring required:
MORE WORK + LESS REWARD = DISSATISFACTION

Market forces are exerting tremendous pressure on businesses to reduce costs and preserve bottom-line profits. In medicine, this is especially true for large, top-heavy organizations such as hospitals, large independent provider groups, and corporations. Employees begin to feel they are being cheated or taken advantage of somehow. This is precisely what is happening in the healthcare industry.

Salaries have stagnated as reimbursements have fallen or failed to keep up with inflation, taxes, fees, and mandates. Salary increases have become fewer and farther between.

Job benefits have taken a beating as cutbacks are enlisted to strengthen the bottom line. The cost of employee healthcare is being shifted to employees as high-deductible plans are adopted to save money. In this regard, the healthcare benefit is beginning to look more like a liability.

Large companies once flush with management personnel, are now actively eliminating middle management positions. Those responsibilities are being shifted to the ranks without a change in job title or any attendant prestige. This effectively reduces possibilities for career advancement.

With less possibility for advancement, there is less opportunity to expand one's expertise in a given area of endeavor. This effect is compounded as more autonomy is taken from the individuals in the workforce in lieu of more centralized control. Job theaters become more restrictive, less innovative, less creative, and most importantly, less productive.

Long gone are the days when one would begin work for a company at a low wage when young, work for thirty or forty years, see a steady rise in salary and position, then retire with a pension. Bankruptcy, downsizing, layoffs, and restructuring efforts have all but eliminated this once-familiar scenario, which has crushed the notion of job security.

All of this, all of these various actions and reactions, only serve to increase employee dissatisfaction, contributing heavily to employee burnout even as intrinsic value evaporates. Large and small employers alike must eventually come to understand that a burned out workforce will cost more in the long run than cost-cutting measures such as these will ever save. You can bank on it.

What's tragic is it just doesn't have to be this way. Much can be done to reward workers and those in management and recognize them for their hard work without breaking the bank. The best way to create a bottom line surplus is with a fully engaged workforce.

#4. Breakdown of Community

As organizations grow larger or too quickly, a breakdown in the character of the organization can result as short-term profit is chased at the expense of interpersonal relationships within the company. This will inevitably lead to greater conflicts among employees, a lack of mutual support, lack of respect, and a growing sense of isolation.

Dr. Maslach states, "A sense of belonging disappears when people work separately instead of together." In the presence of growing isolation, you will find the absence of a sense of community. Hospitals, large provider groups, clinics, companies, agencies, organizations, universities, and churches each represent, in and of themselves, a community. The strength of these organizations is derived from the strength of the interpersonal relationships formed within each of them.

If a community is thriving, the interpersonal relationship bonds are strong within that community. Wherever and whenever the sense of community breaks down, you will find burned-out employees.

Interpersonal relationships are a fundamental component of community within an organization. One of the top reasons people look forward to going to work is because of the anticipated social interaction with their fellow employees. This makes work more interesting, fosters teamwork, and provides a platform for mutual support.

Unfortunately, in some organizations employees can become so isolated they may know little or nothing about the professional and personal lives of their fellow coworkers even three or four cubicles over. Let alone one or two floors up or down.

I once spoke to a group of radiologists where some partners had either just come on board or had been there for decades, with every age bracket in between represented. One of the senior partners, privately voicing his frustration, was annoyed with one of the younger radiologists who always seemed to be late in for work or running behind. I would find out later that no one else in the entire group knew the younger radiologist had a special-needs child at home and was struggling on many levels. He had not felt welcome to share his pain or his burden with his partners. There was no sense of community within this group. It shouldn't be this way.

Where employee turnover is high, whether due to cost-cutting measures or to a poor work environment, job security is further eroded. Without job security, tight interpersonal relationships cannot be formed. Any sense of community is either lost in this way or is unable to fully develop.

The meme, "We are all in this together," is replaced by, "It's every man and women for themselves." I ask you: can a quality a product or service be produced if this is the prevailing attitude within an organization?

To review, here are seven reasons why breakdown of community will either ruin your business or burn you out:

1. Creates conflict.
2. Undermines teamwork.
3. Communication breakdown.
4. The sense of belonging disappears.
5. Loss of support and respect.
6. Growing sense of isolation.
7. Loss of job security.

Many positive steps can be taken to repair a damaged sense of community or to create a sense of community where none yet exists. It requires making the work environment conducive to building interpersonal relationships among your fellow employees. I have developed an eBook entitled, *An Apple A Day Gets the Employee to Stay: 50 Low Cost or No Cost Ways to Keep Employees Happy!* The suggestions in this little eBook can go a long way toward correcting the job-employee mismatches of insufficient reward and breakdown of community that can lead to burnout. If you are a business owner, an office administrator, or if you're a burned-out employee and would like to pass along a copy to your employer, download your copy now absolutely FREE at http://ReigniteBook.com/an-apple-a-day-gets-the-employee-to-stay/.

If you are a physician, PA, FNP, nurse, a group or hospital administrator, you can download the FREE eBook, *An Apple A Day Gets the Provider to Stay: 50 Low Cost or No Cost Ways to Keep your Providers Happy!* Go to ClarkGaither.com and claim your copy now.

#5. Absence of Fairness

A few years ago, just before retiring, a friend told me she was fired as a pharmaceutical representative after twenty-seven years with the same company. There were massive layoffs within her company as they attempted to cost-cut their way to a better bottom line. As a result, I can tell you firsthand that 100 percent of those who remained with her company became cynical and burned out and did so almost overnight. Many who remained began to jump ship.

This story personifies the fifth job-employee mismatch that causes burnout: absence of fairness.

Over the years, I have had many pharmaceutical representatives call on my office. There used to be many reps touting twenty, twenty-five, and thirty or more years with their company. When asked how long they would continue to work, all would tell me they would happily work for their company until the day they retired. Most of them had at least some gray hair.

Sadly, as the healthcare environment and the pharmaceutical industry began to change, most of the older representatives were let go because of cost cutting measures, reorganizations, or mergers, many just before retirement. This is why those who remained behind burned out so quickly. Who can blame them?

Today, most of the pharmaceutical representatives who come to my office are in their twenties or early thirties, and they switch companies often. Few of the "gray hairs" remain. This kind of corporate purging is seen as tremendously unfair. The result: rampant industry-wide employer distrust. I hear it every day.

Many other industries across the country have employed these same tactics. In addition, less productive and inefficient employees are retained while the "last hired" are let go, only to be hired back as contract workers at less pay in order to fix the problems those left behind cannot fix. Or full-time employees are made into part-time employees to save money on salary and benefits. All of these scenarios create a sense of absence of fairness, leading to an embittered, burned-out workforce.

Most Americans carry with them a sense of fairness. We want to see people treated fairly, we want to treat people fairly, and we want to be treated fairly. This is ingrained in most of us from an early age. We feel uneasy, even distressed, when we see fairness being disregarded or violated. Nowhere is this more true and obvious than in the workplace.

In her book *The Truth About Burnout*, Dr. Christina Maslach asserts that, "A workplace is perceived to be fair when three key elements are present: *trust, openness, and respect.*" In her studies, she found all three of these elements to be essential in order for an employee to feel valued and engaged (the opposite of burnout) at work. In direct contrast, the absence of any of these three key elements will contribute directly to job-related burnout.

You can know when a sense of fairness is being eroded within an organization when you begin to notice the following:

- When an organization begins to take actions with little concern or input from employees.
- When short-term financial performance is sought in lieu of building organizational community.
- When management no longer takes staff members' assessments of services and problems at face value.
- When staff are viewed as being primarily concerned with protecting their job more than the welfare of customers, patients, or clients.
- When open and honest communication is no longer a priority or even sought.
- When management begins to value secrecy more than openness.
- When management changes the parameters or modes of operation without any explanation.

- When organizations restructure (hiring entry-level employees and letting go of/forcing early retirement on experienced, salaried employees) to cut costs.
- When organizations forgo raises and/or employee benefits with the excuse they cannot be afforded, yet increase the compensation packages or pay out large bonuses to those in management.

The uneven and unfair distribution of rewards is probably the single most important impediment to building a sense of community among employees. This will undermine and destroy the development of productive relationships with fellow co-workers.

You know, it just doesn't have to be this way. Much can be done to instill in employees the sense of trust and feelings of openness and respect necessary to build community and avoid burnout.

#6. Conflicting Values

Everyone has a set of core values that guide them in life and in their everyday interactions with others. If you work for an organization, you bring those values with you into the workplace. The creation of conflicting values in the workplace can put employees on the fast track to job burnout.

If an organization such as a large hospital or provider group touts excellent service or always placing the patient first, but behind the scenes the employees know this is not true, then substantial internal conflict will arise. This can be extremely frustrating and demoralizing to the employees, especially if their internal moral compass or core values are being assailed. To achieve a quality product or service, a company's values must remain in alignment with those of the employees.

Of all the mismatches between the nature of a job and the nature of the person doing the job, conflicting values probably carry the most weight. If individuals find themselves in a job where there is substantial conflict between the demands of the job and their core values, there will exist great potential for job burnout.

Now, most organizations do not go out of their way to create value conflicts. This is often unplanned and can happen very innocently.

Organizations may emphasize dedicated and excellent service but inadvertently take steps that actually destroy their ability to deliver a quality product or service. While attempting to improve customer service, greater distance can be put between the patient, client, or customer and the organization. Examples are automated phone menus, teller machines, information kiosks, online-only ordering, patient information portals, etc. Shorter wait times are great, but they come at the expense of face time with human employees.

Consider this: if you are the customer, client, or patient and have a problem or a complaint, would you want to be directed to an online questionnaire or would you prefer to sit down and voice the issue with another human being? The online questionnaire might be more expeditious for the organization, but does it really demonstrate next-level quality or service?

In her book *The Truth About Burnout*, Dr. Christina Maslach identified four primary guiding values for excellence in customer service: be efficient, be accurate, be personal, and be adaptable to the individual. Does this sound like many large businesses today? No matter how great an organization's value statement may sound, it isn't worth the paper it is printed on if each of these guiding values is not fully addressed in the everyday course of business. If there is conflict between an organization's stated values and the organization's performance, the employees will take notice and so will the people they serve.

We have also recently seen a glaring example where an organization publicly stated it cared, while behind the scenes overtly demonstrated how it couldn't have cared less. I'm talking about the VA healthcare scandal of 2014.

People were being purposefully lied to in order to make certain internal metrics look good while actively projecting the persona of: "We care very deeply about our veterans, but we are just too short-staffed and lack necessary resources to see you in the most timely manner."

How many great, competent, and caring staff did the VA frustrate, burn out, or lose over the years because behind the scenes the truth was known to them? Those who could not abide the internal conflicts this situation created simply left.

How many labored on, not knowing the truth, hoping that something would change, doing their best under the circumstances but unable to deliver their best work to the veterans for which they cared so deeply? This was a tragedy for them as well.

Any who remained and actively participated in this sham showed their internal values to be on par with the hideous lies they told. Hence, as amoral as they were, they saw no conflict between themselves and the organization.

You know what? It just doesn't have to be this way. There are many steps an organization can take to ensure the values they espouse are true and emulate the values of the workforce.

Do you feel the values of the organization for which you work reflect your own internal values? Do you know your top ten core values and your #1 core value? If not, I will give you a free tool to determine them later on in this book.

Bottom Line

These mismatches can occur in any combination or in aggregate. However, they must each be addressed individually, as each will have a unique set of solutions. The costs of job-related burnout are devastatingly high, not only for the individual employee but any organization as a whole.

Failure to address these mismatches will result in a dysfunctional and burned-out staff with high staff turnover and inferior products or services. I will be discussing each of these individual job mismatches along with what can be done to lessen their impact or eliminate them altogether.

Do you recognize any of these mismatches in your current work environment? In yourself? If so, have you thought about what to do about them?

If you feel you or your organization may be suffering from the effects of job-related burnout, there is much which can be done to mitigate, alleviate, or eliminate these symptoms simply by identifying and addressing these underlying causes.

YOUR PREFERRED FUTURE

ndividuals who are burning out or burned out are often paralyzed by indecision, unable to move forward or backward. Even a lateral move seems impossible or, at the very least, an ineffective solution. They feel completely trapped by their circumstances. When I was writing this book, I was reminded of when I was in Arizona in 2014, hiking in the red rock canyons surrounding Sedona. Just outside of the city, at the top of Bear Mountain, I found the remains of a burned tree. It was ash gray and lifeless but still sturdy and standing.

Perhaps it had been severely burned by wildfire, or it could have succumbed silently to disease or some other change in the environment. No matter. I snapped a picture. Later, as I was going over my photos for the day, the tree struck me as a symbol, a symbol for burnout.

When I was suffering from burnout, I didn't feel alive, but I was still standing, working in spite of my emotional, mental, physical, and spiritual exhaustion. I could no longer visualize other, better possibilities for myself. I saw no avenues leading to change, only roadblocks. I was truly stuck.

It is hard to muster the energy to change, to upend your work life or personal life and escape burnout, if you are exhausted. Burnout clouds the thinking and erodes resolve. Burnout limits choices by engendering fear.

The hardest part of effecting needed change is simply entertaining the notion that real, meaningful, and positive change is even possible. The fear that stands in the way can be set aside, but it takes intentional effort. For some, it will be an act of desperation that sets fear aside.

Desperation is the least desirable impetus for change if you are burned out. Decisions made in desperation are not often the best decisions. In desperation there is little time for logical reasoning (ratiocination), planning, or deliberative action.

In desperation, someone may give up on their life's calling, just because of a bad work environment. This is most certainly just the beginning of another burnout tragedy leading to a life unfulfilled and a lifetime of unhappiness.

It just doesn't have to be this way. If you are burned out or feeling burned out, know this—although the tree I found at the top of that mountain had no options for changing its circumstances, people do. We all have choices, always.

You don't have to just stand there and take it until you die. Your greatest potential is waiting to be unleashed. Take the first step toward reigniting with passion and purpose.

Begin by acknowledging you are in need of change, then commit to picking up the tools, information, and resources necessary to make your preferred future a reality. Don't just stand there. Get moving.

Taking Responsibility

Yes, I've been burned out. When I was burned out, everything looked dismal to me. My outlook was terrible. I traded optimism for pessimism at every turn. Everyone around me began to annoy me. I blamed the way I felt on them. It didn't make me feel any better. It only made things worse.

One day, I had had enough. I was tired of making the world my enemy. It wasn't getting me anywhere anyway. I decided to make some changes. I decided to take control of my circumstances and make the task of improving them my responsibility.

Things got better, immensely better. It was then I realized I was responsible for what had happened to me. Sure, my work environment was certainly conducive to burnout, but I hadn't done anything to circumvent it from happening or to escape from its clutches.

Even before I realized I was burned out, I languished feeling that way far too long before taking needed actions because it was easier to stay miserable and blame someone else for the way I was feeling. I didn't want to take responsibility for my own feelings.

I was reminded of all this recently when a friend of mine, Casie, was talking about assigning blame by finger pointing. She said, "Someone once showed me when you point your index finger at someone else, you have three fingers pointing right back at yourself."

This is not only true in reality; it is true in principle. Most of the time when we begin to assign blame to others, we become clueless as to what role or part we played. We fail to accept responsibility for our own actions or inactions that contributed to the undesirable outcome.

I have done this countless times in the past. It was easy to do. I didn't want to be wrong or at fault. Making someone else to blame for a mess I created not only absolved me of blame but also of the responsibility for cleaning up the mess.

It was all designed to help me to feel better about myself. I may have felt better while doing this, but it wasn't making me any better as a person. Ultimately, it was self-defeating.

It is true; we cannot control the actions of other people when they are making decisions that directly affect us as individuals. Not every bad or undesired outcome is our fault or our responsibility. It is likewise incorrect to assume every bad or undesired outcome is never our fault or responsibility. What is always 100-percent our responsibility is how we react to a bad or undesired outcome, no matter if we are the cause or if someone else is responsible.

It has taken me most of my life to realize that accepting responsibility for a failure doesn't make me a failure. Making mistakes doesn't make you a bad person. It makes you human. Everyone makes mistakes. Mistakes are how we learn and grow, if we choose.

Let's say you're experiencing a bad outcome, like burnout, which is affecting you either directly or indirectly. Rather than automatically assigning blame, which saps energy and solves nothing, ask yourself the following questions:

- What decisions did I make or actions did I take that led directly to the undesired outcome?
- Were there inactions on my part that lead to the undesired outcome?
- What could I have done to ensure a better, different, or more desirable outcome?
- If I was not responsible for the undesirable outcome, what decisions can I make or actions can I take to make things right or better?
- Can I find a way to be grateful for what has happened, and what lessons can I take away from the experience?

I believe asking these basic questions when things are not going your way will lead to a happier and more peaceful existence, one imbued with self-awareness and marked by personal growth.

Do You Know What You Want?

I had always felt that eventually everything would come together. I thought one day, one night, success would come in one clear moment. In one clear moment, I would know I had arrived, and in an instant all I ever wanted in life would come to me.

So, I planned and worked, planned and worked harder, waiting for the one clear moment that would guarantee my success forever yet never knowing what it would be or when it might come. There is just one problem: It never happened that way. It never does.

I lived this way for a long time, hopscotching through life from one idea to the next, one project to the next, one career to the next, expecting the one clear moment to reveal itself. I felt like I was chasing something elusive. It felt elusive because I lacked clarity and focus on exactly what I was after.

I remember concentrating a good bit on how I felt going through a good many years and a hodgepodge of efforts. Do you know what concentrating on my feelings got me? Nothing and nowhere. At least that is how I felt. There it is again—feelings.

It took a personal tragedy to startle me out of my old paradigm, the one which wasn't working, the one without well-defined goals. It took a cold bracer of reality to slap some sense into me. I was in my late fifties, successful by many measures, but feeling totally lost—not only lost, but directionless and lacking a sense of purpose and passion.

I began to ask myself the hard questions: Who am I? Where am I headed? Why am I doing this? What do I really want? Something shifted. Something awakened. A fire reignited and began to burn deep inside. I began to search for the answers to the hard questions, something I had never done before.

In a TED talk Mel Robbins famously said: "I don't care how you feel. I care about what you want. If you listen to how you feel, when it comes to what you want you will not get it because you will never feel like it."

My feelings often told me things like: "I'm too tired," "I can't do that," "It's too late for me," "I'm not good enough," "I don't know how," "I don't have the right degree," "It will take too long," "It will cost too much," or "No one will like it."

I never felt like doing what I needed to do, to take the time and put in the effort to figure out exactly what I wanted and how to get it. I let my feelings get in the way.

Have you ever felt this way? If so, allow me to share with you the benefit of some hard-learned lessons.

Set aside the self-indulgent, minute-to-minute, hour-to-hour, day-to-day analysis of how you feel. I believe answering this basic question, "What precisely is it that I want?" will make the biggest difference in your life. Knowing exactly what you want will help you to drop the excuses. That is, if you don't allow your feelings to hold you back.

It may take some time to discover the answer. It's okay. The search is imperative. It can be the difference between a life of purpose-driven passion and fulfillment and a life of seemingly endless wandering and searching for "I don't know what." Everyone would like their own measure of success. If you don't know what you want, how will you ever know when you get it?

Eight Truths About Your Journey

We are all familiar with the thematic metaphor of life as a journey. All of us are walking an unfamiliar path toward an uncertain future. That does not mean we have no influence on our futures. At one time, I used to believe in destiny, one in which I had little choice or input. That belief precluded me from taking any personal responsibility for my actions or for what happened to me as a consequence of my actions.

Living under those circumstances required little effort on my part because whatever was to happen was going to happen. I was just along for the ride. These notions were insidiously alluring.

Personal tragedy caused my belief system to change. It had to if I were to gain any measure of control over my life, which seemed completely out of my control. I say "seemed" because such was my belief system; however, believing I had no control was a choice from the outset. Therefore, I was always in control. I chose to believe that way because I didn't feel I deserved any better.

As I said, my belief system changed. Oh, I still believe in destiny, just not in the same way. I believe we can seek out our own destiny or, at the very least, have the greatest influence on our own destiny if we choose.

If life is a journey, then we are all on a particular path, paths with many branches, dead ends, switchbacks, descents, ascensions, and barriers both real and perceived. Through sixty years of living, I have learned several truths about the paths we walk.

- **Truth #1.** It took me a long time to come to this first absolute, and in my case, sobering truth. I get to decide on which path I will walk. I chose the path. The path does not choose me. No one decides for me, not without my permission. No one decides for you which path you will walk. We all choose for ourselves.

- **Truth #2.** You can just stand on your path and refuse to budge, but you will advance anyway. Time's arrow points in but one direction—forward. If you do not move forward, time will sweep you and the path on which you stand forward and on into the future, with or without your permission. Everything around you will change, even if you do not. It is best to have some say in which forward direction you're headed.

- **Truth #3.** Our time here is limited. If you haven't fulfilled your earthly purpose, you must begin your search now. If you are searching for your earthly purpose but haven't yet found it, just keep searching. It may be just around the next bend, just up ahead. If you have found your earthly purpose, you are on the right path, the one which is true for you.

- **Truth #4.** If you run into an obstacle or barrier to your progress, you must remove it or find a way over, under, or around it. No one will do this for you, at least not for very long. Those who may stop to help you will ultimately give in to their own concerns at some point and leave to continue their own journey. Don't hold them back. That is not your purpose.

- **Truth #5.** Although some may seem closed, all paths are open. They all begin from where you are, where you stand. They branch out in every direction without limit. They are constantly changing and refreshing in front of you. Don't forget to look up. There are paths there too.

- **Truth #6.** People will come in and out of our lives as we walk our paths. Our paths may cross, overlap, or parallel one another for a little while, but they will never be the same. No one will journey with us at all times, nor will we journey with them for all time.

- **Truth #7.** Your journey will never provide all that you want but will always provide all of your needs if you accept them. The needs that are provided may come disguised as mistakes, failure, struggle, loss, and hardship. Sometimes, so too will rewards.

- **Truth #8.** This is the most startling and astonishing one of them all. If all paths lead away from you in all directions, then they must also lead to you from all directions. To me, this is profound. Although we walk different paths, they are all connected. Be open to opportunities. They will come to you every day from many different directions. Most will be difficult to recognize. At all times, be aware.

It is both exciting and comforting to me that I can influence the final outcome of my journey by the paths I choose and the decisions I make along the way. So can you. So should you. What a gift.

Do you feel you are in control of the path you are on, your journey? Do you know where you are headed? Do you wish for a change in direction?

Ten Suggestions for Reality-Based Living

A patient once told me, "I used to sit a lot and think a lot about success. I would sit and sit and think and think. But success never came my way. I halfway expected it to come and knock on my door and present itself to me like a carefully wrapped package. Boy, was I ever wrong!"

He went on to tell me how he eventually made success happen. First, he wrote down what success would look like to him. Second, he formulated a plan to get what he wanted. Third, he got to work and began to take action steps, which moved him toward his goals. Since then, he has enjoyed monumental success in the manufacturing sector. No, it wasn't overnight success either. It never is.

I have encountered many people in my career with all kinds of dreams. There are those who were able to attain their dreams by following the three steps outlined above. Too many others have never realized their dreams, and most never will.

They depend on dreaming, luck, chance, being good, suffering, marriage, prayer, associations, instructional books, seminars, instructional videos, the right time, clubs, partying, the educational system, degrees, and many other success promising enticements and inducements to make them successful.

These are non-strategy strategies with no basis in reality. They strictly avoid steps 1, 2, and 3 above.

People are, by and large, hopeful for their futures. If you are not hopeful for your future, meaning you are feeling hopeless, then there is little reason to get out of bed in the morning.

We hope and pray for many things. Commonly hoped for things include love, health, ubiquitous stuff, a fulfilling job, passion, or purpose. We hope and pray for these things in order to bring added meaning to our lives.

But many never realize their dreams and never obtain what they truly desire. Why? Is it because of a lack of luck, bad timing, a lack of faith, not the right education, a lack of money, an unsupportive spouse? I do not believe so.

We have amazing bodies with a complex and highly functional brain to boot. Each of us is born with unique talents and abilities. If we feel something is missing, we have the wherewithal to obtain whatever is lacking.

I believe we have already been given all that we need to succeed in life. For those who are into reality-based belief systems, I submit the following ten suggestions for a more bountiful and successful future:

1. There is no such thing as luck. It is an illusion. Sustained, persistent hard work with passion and purpose will lead to success. To an independent observer, it just looks like luck. It may even look like magic. But it isn't.

2. The concept of overnight success is another mental trap. It infers chance or ease, which is insulting to the person who has worked tirelessly toward their goals, most often over many years, even decades.

3. There is no magic formula, magic wand, or magic fairy dust. There are no shortcuts. There are tried and true formulas for success, which are not magical and are available to anyone. That is, they will work if you work them. Magical thinking gets you zip, zilch, zero. You can read yet another "achieve success quick" scheme or watch another video if you want. How about just picking one and doing it?!

4. Serving the needs, wants, and desires of others will bring you your needs, wants, and desires. They will come from those you serve if you serve them well.

5. If you are full of discontent, unhappiness, and discomfiture and are looking for a sign for when to begin to transform your life, your sign is discontent, unhappiness, and discomfiture.

6. Your preferred future is your dream and no one else's. Translating your life from where you are to your preferred future is your job. No one else will do this for you because they are concerned about their own lives and their own preferred futures.

7. If you say, "I can't," I will not believe you, even though you will be right 100 percent of the time. My not believing it is true will not make any difference though, until you stop believing it is true, at which point you will again be right 100 percent of the time. It is the only instance in your life when you will be 100 percent correct either way. Your choice.

8. Praying for God to do something for you that you can do for yourself, to figure out something that you can figure out for yourself, or to give you something that you can get for yourself, is a waste of mental energy, your natural talents and abilities, not to mention the good Lord's time. Go to work with what you have, what you have been given, and be grateful for it. If it is your opinion that He left you ill-equipped somehow, well then good luck with that conversation.

9. The road to success passes through the gateposts of failure. Every time. Always! There is just no easier, softer way. When you come

to a point where you can name failure as a cherished friend, you will have both feet firmly planted and pointing toward, or actually within, your preferred future.

10. If you use other people simply to get want you want, you will end up with nothing and very few people will want to associate with you. The ones who remain will keep you around just long enough to get what they want from you. (These ten suggestions are an excerpt from my book *POWERFUL WORDS*.)

If you have achieved success, by whatever measure you choose, you are already familiar with the truth of these observations. They have their basis in reality and not fantasy. If instead you have been waiting around for success to pass by you, it does. Every single day. We are glorious creatures of the universe, destined and designed to plan, to accomplish, to build, to produce, to create, to innovate. To be successful.

Do you believe that is true, as I do? Then, welcome to REALVILLE my friend!

The Barrier to Implementing New Ideas Isn't What You Think

How many new business ideas, book ideas, blog posts, services, new products, or works of art have you envisioned but never shipped? I am talking about ideas for great products or services that were never brought to market. One, ten, twenty, hundreds? I would wager, whatever reason or excuse you might offer, it is not the correct one. Many will say new projects never get off the ground due to time constraints, lack of capital, or inadequate expertise. Others may cite a need to procrastinate based on a general lack of support, or because it is just not the right time, or because there is too much competition in the marketplace. I wish it were that simple.

Whether or not we act on an idea is a function of the barriers we erect, not in reality, but between our ears. On the one hand, we have an idea we feel is good enough to act upon based on the merits of the idea alone. One the other hand, we produce a litany of reasons and excuses of why the idea should be postponed or entirely abandoned. It is hardly a fair fight.

But what lies at the heart of it all? Why do we place barriers in our own pathway before we even begin? Is it the cool, calm, and collected head of reason that prevents us from realizing our dreams? Or, something else?

I believe I know. The major barrier to acting on an idea isn't intellectual or even physical. It's emotional.

At the thought of stepping outside our comfort zone we may generate anxiety, doubt, dread, misgiving, phobias, paranoia, trepidation, worry, or outright terror. Underpinning all of these is fear.

The same is true for people deciding whether or not to make a needed change in a particular aspect of their lives, like changing jobs due to burnout, learning a new skill, ending a bad relationship, switching careers, or closing a failing business. Unless you are vigilant, all major decisions will be emotional decisions.

Sure, you can always come up with a plausible explanation as to why something shouldn't be done. Very convincing ones. But, ask yourself this, "Who are you trying to convince and why?" The real why.

It is okay to have these internal "for or against" arguments. In business, it is prudent to be cautious. But beware. Over-cautiousness can be paralyzing. No risk will be accepted if one is too cautious.

Just try to be more aware of the emotional aspects of these internal arguments. If you can remove as much of the emotional component as possible, then you can bring more balance to the decisions you make.

Are your internal arguments over new ideas more intellectual, more emotional, or just about right? Which do you favor? Which has helped you the most? Which has helped you least?

Seven Indicators of Lethal Complacency

I can think of no other force so strong as to keep individuals range bound in variations of sameness throughout their entire lives as effectively as complacency. I guess self-destruction would be worse, but complacency itself is a form of self-destruction.

Complacency is defined as, "*a feeling of quiet pleasure or security, often while unaware of some potential danger, defect, or the like; self-satisfaction or smug satisfaction with an existing situation, condition, etc.*" (Dictionary. com).

Just like the law of Entropy (Δ g), which states systems and matter tend to go from an organized state to one of disorganization and randomness, people can go from a highly adaptable prevailing state of dissatisfaction to abject complacency if they are not perpetually vigilant.

You might say, "Wait a minute. Who lives perpetually dissatisfied? Who would want to?" It's a fair question. I'll tell you who: artists, innovators, entrepreneurs, writers, engineers, designers, singers, actors, CEO's, musicians, and athletes, just to name a few.

To pursue excellence is to be perpetually dissatisfied with the status quo. Complacency is the end of life as you could have known it. Complacency is the lethal enemy of excellence. Don't confuse dissatisfaction with unhappiness.

> "Complacency is the end of life
> as you could have known it."

How is it, then, that so many people sit down in life and accept the comfortable misery of variations in sameness? There are many reasons. Here is an unvarnished, non-PC listing of the seven most common ones.

- Self-Imposed Limitations—The belief you're not good enough or capable. Keywords: "I can't."
- Laziness—Attempting to become content in life looks too much like hard work. Keywords: "I won't."
- Comfortable Misery—Change is feared or considered more painful or difficult than staying put. Keyword: "Slave" (to the status quo)
- Boredom—A state is reached where the sense of wonder and curiosity has been lost. Keywords: "Brain death"
- False Sense of Security and Wellbeing—The mistaken notion that since nothing bad has happened, it never will so I can relax and let my guard down. Keyword: "Delusional"

- Inactivity—A continuous state of feeling too tired to exercise regularly, explore, or try new activities. Keywords: "Couch potato"
- Inattentiveness—We see what we wish to see rather than what is glaringly apparent to everyone else. Keyword: "Fool"

Recognizing complacency is one thing. Doing something about it is quite another. It isn't just a matter of doing the exact opposite of all that causes complacency. It has more to do with adopting a certain lifestyle, a certain attitude. One in which the status quo leads to darkness, and pushing the boundaries of excellence is a stairway to heaven.

Opposite of complacency are concern, interest, discontent, and dissatisfaction. This does not mean you must be unhappy to be non-complacent. You can feel any of these and still be a happy person, for sheer joy is to be found in the remedy for these, in the pursuit of excellence.

To pursue excellence one cannot keep station with the status quo. Convention must be upended. Criticism, even ridicule, must become a real risk. To shun variations in sameness will make many around you uncomfortable with envy, jealousy, and anger.

If you should strike out in the pursuit of excellence, some will do their best to talk you into staying put or even sabotage your efforts to break free of complacency. They will tell you that the road you have chosen is highly unusual. That it will be too hard or that your chances of success are almost zero. They are the complacent ones voicing their dissatisfaction, not with your choices but with their own lives. It is a curious fact that when some see other people succeeding or trying to succeed, they will try to discourage that behavior because it makes them feel better about their decisions to maintain the status quo. In other words, these people perversely feel that because they can't do something or have chosen not to do something, others shouldn't either. A person willing to change, take risk, is threatening to someone stuck in an everyday routine where they feel safe.

All across America, people sit and gawk at flat screen TVs squawking out the latest surreal unreal reality show, never seeking to improve themselves by reading a book, taking a course, learning a new skill, visiting a museum, traveling to an unknown destination, starting a new business, putting brush to canvas or pen to paper.

They are the socially-engineered, totally complacent, and acceptable carbon-copy zombies of the status quo. We need not wait for the zombie apocalypse. It is already upon us. Fear promises nothing. I should know. I used to be one of them.

If you are reading this now, please tell me you are not one who favors complacency. If you are, it is never too late to make something happen. Life is short, too short for bystander status. You can upgrade your living status at any time, and it's free. All you need do is become dissatisfied with the status quo and willing to do something about it.

If you are already in the continuous pursuit of excellence, then you are engaged in the truest pursuit of happiness. It's the quiet dissatisfaction you harbor for the status quo which drives you forward in the service of others using your unique set of natural talents and abilities. Complacency will never claim your life, as long as you are vigilant.

The Minimalist Guide to Indecision

There you are, stuck. Or, so you feel. Afraid to leave the soul-sucking job for a better life, even though you know you are completely burned out. Afraid to move out, afraid to move in. Afraid to lean in, afraid to lean back. So, on it goes.

Of course, the basis of this lack of prudent decisiveness is fear. The emotion, fear, is hardwired into every human brain. It has served a vital role for our survival as a species. No one is fearless. It is a powerful emotion we all share.

The brain would just as soon suffer ongoing misery from a place of perceived safety than the thought of an unknown outcome from a different venture, risk, business decision, relationship, job, or career. Some have termed this state comfortable misery. It's not comfortable, but it is misery, nonetheless.

Comfortable misery is only perceived as safe because it is what is known. It is not a safe place in which to live. The fact is, it is a very dangerous place in which to live. Comfortable misery causes us to eat up the one commodity we are all running short of: time.

Fearing that change might be worse than what currently exists, take more energy or require more money can coerce one into a state of benign resignation. So, people become stuck, sometimes paralyzed, by fear. Fear promises nothing. I say forget that. Life is too short.

How does one get past this block, this thing that feels like an impenetrable wall when decisions for our better interest need to be made? Like most situations in life where the human brain is concerned, there are no easy answers, everyone's path is different. I will tell you what will help you to overcome fear of needed change. Let start with this quote by Usman B. Asif, "Fear is a darkroom where negatives develop." Absolutely true. Scary things are much scarier in the dark.

Overcoming fear is not about becoming fearless. It's about bringing the negatives out into the light. We don't have to struggle with the big, or even the little, problems in absolute darkness or silence.

Find people you trust and share your struggle with them. Telling what you fear the most to another human being will lessen the impact of the fear of the unknown. Hearing someone else's story about how they dealt with a similar situation will have a liberating effect. This is the primary reason we have language, to share what we know for mutual benefit and for survival.

If needed, get professional help through counseling or coaching. This is your life. Your story. Hopefully, many chapters have yet to be written. Be the author of your own story. With each passing day and each turn of the page, you can decide how your story unfolds.

Do We Seize the Moment, or Does the Moment Seize Us?

You have been there. I know you have. Everyone has. The one clear moment when everything fell into place or came crashing down. A moment where, in an instant, you knew something important happened, something shifted.

It was a moment you will remember forever. Perhaps it was when you had a personal epiphany. Or perhaps it was when someone else took an action which greatly affected you, something completely out of your control. Someone said something or someone did something that changed your life forever.

Perhaps something wonderful happened. Something that created such joy and happiness you felt it could never be repeated. Those are the easiest moments to hang onto and the hardest to let go.

No matter. There you were—right place, right time. Or, wrong place, wrong time. You had a life-altering realization or event and you knew your life would never be the same, and it never was.

Did you seize that moment, or did the moment seize you? It depends, as they say, on your perspective.

I don't believe in chance when it comes to humans. It's too random for me. I don't believe in fate either. There are no options when it comes to fate. I believe in LIFE and the endless and limitless possibilities it provides. I believe in choice.

We all make choices. Some good. Some neutral or indifferent. Some bad. Although there are different kinds of choices, all choices have one thing in common: CONSEQUENCES.

Some people experience life-changing moments that they should let go of immediately, or as soon as possible, and forever but never do. As in moments of tragedy, heartbreak, illness, misfortune, or accident they become stuck. In doing so, I believe they have allowed the moment to seize them.

I've been stuck before. I have had moments in my past I have held onto way past their natural expiration dates. Some I held onto like grim death for years and years. I have allowed past moments to seize me, from which there was no recovery. There was no going back because I never moved forward. Not until I let go.

Other moments I seized for myself rather than allowing them to seize me. Like the moment a customer in a Radio Shack I was managing said to me, "Sounds like you can do anything you make up your mind to do." I enrolled in college the very next day and later became a family physician.

There was the moment when a patient asked me what I was doing for cardiovascular exercise after I had just berated him for his lack of the same.

The truth was, I wasn't doing anything. I bought running clothes that same evening and began running. I have been running ever since, some 16 years later. My physical, emotional, mental, and spiritual realms have all improved as a result.

There was the moment I realized I had become burned out in my career. I had experienced most of the six mismatches between the job and the individual that can cause burnout. Instead of just sucking it up or quitting, I decided to make some needed changes. It made all the difference in the way I feel about medicine. In finding a way to help myself, I have discovered ways I can help other professionals suffering from job burnout.

There was the moment when I found out my wife was leaving me. To say I was devastated would be a gross understatement. But I decided I wasn't going to self-destruct and things would get better with time. Things did get better with time. Much better. Astonishingly better.

I took that moment to change a lot of other things about my life. I began new journeys. Some have concluded. Others are ongoing. The transformation has been, in a word, amazing!

The way I see it, I believe there are just two possible outcomes for our life-changing moments. You can allow the moment to seize you. Or, you can seize the moment. Either way, there will be consequences. Either way, it is a choice.

As I said before, I believe in choice. Do you?

Have there been times in your life where you have allowed the moment to seize you? Have there been times you distinctly remember seizing the moment?

Success Rubs Off, But Only Onto Those in the Nearby Vicinity

You have heard it before. If you want to be successful, surround yourself with successful people. This often-repeated statement happens to be true, which is why it is often repeated. There is sound observational science to back up this claim. Whatever it may be successful people possess, it rubs off on those around them.

Dr. Albert Bandura, a preeminent psychologist, developed a social behavioral theory called Social Cognitive Theory (SCT). Briefly and in summary, the theory posits:

- An individual's acquisition of knowledge is directly related to observing others.
- Human survival depends on the emulation of the successful actions of others.
- People do not learn behaviors just by trying them and either succeeding or failing.
- When people observe a behavior and all of the attendant consequences, they will remember the sequence of events of the behavior and use the information in their own behaviors afterwards.
- Observing a behavior can prompt an individual to engage in behavior they have already learned.
- Depending on whether people are rewarded or punished for the behavior and the final outcome of the behavior, people will choose whether or not to replicate the behavior.

There you have it. We are influenced by the behaviors of the people with whom we associate. If we surround ourselves with positive, strong, motivated, and successful people, we will tend to model their behavior.

If we should surround ourselves with whining, complaining, negative, and largely unsuccessful people…Well, you get the point! When I was an active alcoholic, I surrounded myself with people who liked to drink as much as I did—partly to justify my own level of alcohol consumption and partly because I didn't think I deserved any better. The thing is, because of the choices I was making, I didn't deserve any better. My posse and I were all headed nowhere fast.

Once I broke free of my addiction to alcohol, I began to seek better for myself. At first, this included being around people who were successful in recovery. After a while, it included people who were successful in business and living a life they chose to live.

A few years ago, I decided to see what else I might be able to accomplish in this world and began to try new things, to stretch myself beyond what I thought I was capable of doing. I began writing. I started a podcast. I eventually joined a community of successful entrepreneurs and ended up in a Mastermind group. The results have been amazing.

If you want to succeed at what you do, to seek a higher level, to stretch beyond your own borders of the safe, the tried, and the predictable, then seek out successful people and begin to learn from them. This will provide you with opportunities to be both challenged and held accountable for your plans and actions.

Don't worry that you can't or won't be able to contribute to the successful people with whom you choose to associate. You will. We all have different skill sets, knowledge bases, and resources available to us. Someone will benefit from what you already know.

Vigorous personal growth requires fertile ground. Look around you. Are you standing in the tall grass or on barren soil?

Sometimes You Just Have to Hit RESTART

I met a colleague once who confided in me there was one point in his life when he had become completely and hopelessly burned out. Not only had he contemplated quitting his career in medicine, he had even contemplated the ultimate bow-out—suicide. He wasn't just burned out over his job; he had become burned out on living.

How does someone get to a point such as this, that it is better to die than to go on living because of one's feelings, something which can change? He had hit all three of the hallmarks of burnout—emotional exhaustion, cynicism, and inefficacy. One should never underestimate the effects of these powerful negative forces on the human psyche.

He came to feel utterly used up, spent, that he had nothing left to give to anyone. He had become overly pessimistic and distrusting of people, holding everyone around him in contempt. He felt ineffectual in everything he did, like a complete failure in his profession and in life.

Anybody who knew him would have been dismayed over hearing this. Here was a professional, at the pinnacle of his career with seemingly everything in the world going for him. He possessed great intelligence. He had a great job, a loving family, status in the community, economic stability, and was well-liked. None of that mattered to him because of how he was feeling.

He was trying his best to hide his true feelings because he was ashamed of them. He felt he should be able to handle anything, much like most men, much like most physicians.

His work environment was the source of his discontent, not his career. Terrible mismatches had been created between the job he was asked to do and his own internal values. This is what led to his burnout.

One day, out of desperation, he quit his job. He said it was either quit or put a gun to his head and pull the trigger. He walked out after leaving a two-word note on his desk: "I quit!"

Quitting a job where you are feeling burned out isn't the only option available. Sometimes the work environment can be changed to alleviate burnout. In his case, the circumstances of his employment wouldn't allow for the changes necessary for him to stay. So, he left.

He took time off and spent some of it traveling. He began to meditate and see to his other personal needs—physical, emotional, and spiritual. This served to improve and support his overall mental status. He started feeling better. Much better.

He got back in touch with his core values. Although he loved his profession, he vowed never again to put his values in jeopardy over a job. He took responsibility for what he could do to change the way he felt. He took a new job. One that was more closely aligned with his core values. Where once he was merely surviving, he was now thriving.

Today, if you were to ask him how he feels, he would most likely say something like, "On top of the world" because that is honestly how he feels these days. He let his old job change him into thinking he could adapt. He couldn't. When he changed his work environment, he changed the way he felt about himself, his profession, his colleagues, his family, his patients, the world, and life.

He decided to become the captain of his own ship. Tragically, too many people who are burning out, or burned out, labor on under the notion nothing can change. Well, feelings can and do change. Sometimes you just have to hit restart.

Are you honoring your core values? Do you know your top five core values or your #1 core value? If not, there is a FREE Core Values Inventory (CVI) assessment available for download at http://ReigniteBook.com/the-core-values-inventory/. Go and get your copy now.

Don't Wait for Just the Right Time

I have said it before, and I will say it again. I have spent too much of my life waiting. Waiting is a form of procrastination. In my case, it wasn't to avoid work. I have always worked hard at whatever interests me. Rather, for me, it was more of a form of delayed self- actualization manifested by waiting for just the right time.

I have waited until just the right time to start new projects. I have waited until just the right time to take trips to faraway places. I have waited until the absolute, ideal, just right time to begin or launch a new product or service.

At least, that is what I told myself. I now know this behavior was just an excuse to circumvent fear, anxiety, lack of commitment, poor preparation, or perceived inadequacies. Although, looking back, lack of commitment seemed to be the impetus behind most of my waiting for just the right time.

The problem with this is far too often the right time never comes. The new project doesn't get started or completed, the grand trip or adventure is never taken, the new idea or product is never launched.

I convinced myself I was waiting for inspiration. I have negotiated with myself to wait until I felt more rested. I have argued with myself that I should wait until I have more money on hand or that I should read another book, or take another class, or purchase another instructional webinar series. You know, until the time was just right.

There were times I needed to do some hard work on me, personal work. There were times I needed to leave a toxic relationship or an atrocious work environment where I was burning out. However, I chose not to do so because it just wasn't the right time.

By waiting for just the right time, I effectively forfeited having new learning and growth experiences. I denied myself the potential pleasure of glowing success and the valuable lessons of failure. Ultimately, I missed out on golden opportunities to be of value to others.

Besides, what does the "right time" mean anyway? Do the things we wish to do come with a checklist that must be completed before we can begin, or is it just some nebulous construct of a notion we generate in our own heads to temporarily make ourselves feel better for not taking immediate action?

How do we know when the right time becomes available other than another feeling? Is that our supreme and infallible test for the right time, when we feel like it? Or does a popup appear somewhere in our visual field that reads GO? Does the man behind the curtain shout BEGIN? Or do we simply reach a point where we have exhausted all of our excuses?

Worse yet, how many times do humans just forget about their high hopes, sterling ideals, trailblazing ideas, amazing potential, and possibilities because it never was just the right time?

How much innovation has been lost but for waiting for just the right time? How much pain and suffering would have been eliminated but for waiting for just the right time? How much individual joy and pleasure would have been created and conveyed to others but for waiting for just the right time?

Let's be honest here. Each of us already knows just the right time to bind with happiness, secure our families, rise up, use our voices, tell our stories, alleviate suffering, heal the sick, comfort the lonely, feed the hungry, eliminate injustice, innovate, create, inspire, teach, learn, grow, and know using our own God-given, unique natural talents and abilities.

It is NOW.

> *"Don't wait. The time will never be just right."*
> **—Napoleon Hill**

Is Your Future the Biggest Gamble of All?

Do you gamble? Most people are not serious gamblers. They would prefer to make better use of their money and time. Some do but purely for the entertainment aspect. A sizable minority of the population is addicted to gambling and will gamble away every last cent they have, even money they don't have.

I look around these days and I notice the unhappiness in people. I hear them complain about the daily grind, how happy they are to have a weekend away from work that they must hate. I can feel the sense of despair over lives that have not turned out the way people had planned and yet....

I see so many individuals addicted to alcohol, prescribed drugs, street drugs, food, and sloth. They complain about how terrible they feel and yet....

I counsel people every day who come to my office and complain about their spouse, their significant other, their children, their parents. Toxic relationships abound where people say they feel trapped, alone, afraid, abused, resentful, and resented, and yet....

Yet people seem loath to change their circumstances, even dire, dangerous, life-threatening circumstances. They stay in situations that exhaust them, rob them of their dignity, and take away hope for a better life. Worse yet, they will let these situations rob them of their preferred future. Why?

I know they have heard that it doesn't have to be that way. I know they know there is help just around every corner. Deep down, they have to know that they are capable of changing things for the better. So, why don't they?

I hear them talk about how things will get better with time. What, by just waiting? I hear them talk about how things will be better next year, yet they have no plans to make things better by this year.

I hear them make excuses for the very same people that they feel are holding them back, and I have to believe that they can't be serious. Yet, they are serious.

They, all of them, are gambling with their futures. They are leaving to chance what should be fiercely, intentionally, and boldly managed—their own lives.

If you know someone like this, or if this sounds like you, then here are five steps any individual can take right now to stop gambling their life away:

- **Make a decision**. Nothing will change for you until you decide it will change. Figuratively speaking, if you don't like the scenery, change the view. You must decide to decide that things will be different. You are at the starting line of the rest of your life, so start moving. You might not know exactly where the finish line is just yet, but at least you will be moving forward. It is much easier to change direction if you are already underway.

- **Help yourself first**. Acknowledge your particular situation. Completely and honestly probe the depth and breadth of it. Know that you can be the agent of change in your own life. Stop waiting for outside forces to rescue you or provide for you. Come to depend on yourself and your own actions for your own needs.

- **Ask for help if needed**. I don't mean a friendly ear to bend or someone that will be content to offer words of encouragement. I mean people, agencies, facilities, providers, institutions, programs, and groups that will offer assistance with your particular issues. This is not in disregard of the second step above. Asking for help if you honestly need it is helping yourself. You may need advice. You may need protection. You may need counseling. You may need treatment. Ask for what you need.

- **Never turn back**. I have seen people extract themselves from deplorable situations only to crawl right back to them in moments of weakness. Protect your weak spots. Develop strategies to protect yourself from the allure of old habits, codependency traps, and those that have harmed you. Your preferred future always lies ahead of you, never behind you.

- **Trust in change**. You must come to realize that you are capable of more, that you can be different, and create, and learn, and produce, and build, and grow. We grow by how we change. We all have different natural talents and abilities that will compel us to change if we choose to use them. If you're not changing, you're not growing.

These steps are just the beginning, to get you moving. They are intended to stop you from gambling away your future, the biggest gamble of all, so you can begin to embrace the possibilities of change. You cannot design your preferred future while simultaneously gambling with it.

Do you feel you have been gambling away your future, just getting by on hopes and dreams? Are there other steps you can take, or have taken, to ensure a more favorable future for yourself?

Why Chance Is Not an Option When It Comes to Your Preferred Future

What does your preferred future look like? Have you thought about it, really thought about it? If you have an exact picture in mind, and you are doing what is necessary right now, then there is a higher likelihood that you will have and live in your preferred future. If not, then you are most likely leaving your future to chance.

Cold Hard Facts: One thing is for sure: success does not follow or favor chance. If you happen to have a clear picture of your preferred future in your mind but have not taken the necessary steps toward attaining and securing that future for yourself, your chances of success are nearly zero.

If you are laboring at a job you detest, spending all you make and saving none, stagnating in an everyday routine that offers nothing but variations of sameness, your chances of a bright and successful future are exactly zero.

If you are addicted to alcohol, another substance, or some habitual behavior, then your chances for a bright and successful future are less than zero.

Your Preferred Future: I see too many people who have come to believe that they are what they are, that they are incapable of change. Nothing could be further from the truth! Sometimes you just have to start over and reshape yourself in order to reshape your life.

The people who do this have undergone a profound and meaningful transformation. They discovered a secret that will work for anyone. They have discovered that transforming is a choice, and they have chosen to choose better for themselves.

Developing the Picture: I believe if we have a clear picture in our minds of our preferred future, then we can reshape ourselves, our lives, to make that picture a reality. That picture must come deep from within.

I love movies. There is an old one that debuted in 1984 and I really enjoyed, the original *Karate Kid*. In the movie Mr. Myiagi (a Japanese karate master and teacher) gets Daniel (his reluctant student) to shape and prune a bonsai tree. Here is some dialogue from a scene in the movie. I believe it is a metaphor for life and living.

> *Daniel objects to Mr. Myiagi's request to prune the bonsai tree, saying, "I don't know how to do this stuff. I may mess it up. I don't want to mess it up!"*
>
> *Mr. Myiagi insists, "Close eye. Trust. Concentrate. Think only tree. Make a perfect picture down to last a'pine needle. Wipe from mind, clean, everything but tree. Nothing exist whole world, only tree. "You got it?" he asks Daniel after a pause.*
>
> *Daniel nods yes with his eyes still closed.*

Mr. Myiagi says to Daniel, "Remember picture?" Daniel replies, "Yeah."

Mr. Myiagi follows, "Make like picture," and hands him some pruning scissors. He says, "Just'a trust'a picture."

Daniel asks, "How do I know if my picture's the right one?"

Mr. Myiagi imparts his wisdom. "If come from inside you, always right one."

Developing a clear image of where you want to be and what you want to do in your preferred future will give you purposeful direction. It must come from inside you, not from somewhere else or someone else.

Transforming the Hopes and Dreams into Reality: It is not enough just to dream. Sure, dreaming is easier than doing, but your dreams are not reality until you make them your reality.

Hope is not a strategy. Only gamblers hope for success. They lose the majority of the time. Las Vegas was built by losers. Las Vegas is owned by planners and doers.

We can transform our lives with continuous positive change. That image of your preferred future is your call to action. It will take a plan, intentional hard work, passion, and perseverance to make it happen.

Along the way you will succeed some, fail a lot, doubt yourself, be tempted to give up, excited one minute and full of dread the next. Straight up, I know of no other easier, softer way. Just trust your picture and start.

Do you have a clear picture of your preferred future? If not, what is holding you back? If so, are you fully engaged in developing that image into reality?

INDIVIDUAL REMEDIES FOR JOB-RELATED BURNOUT

Complete, full-blown burnout can be very difficult to correct—not impossible, but difficult. It is best to avoid this condition at all costs. If prevention is no longer an option and you find you have burned yourself out, there is a way to reignite and do so with powerful passion and purpose.

The REIGNITE Framework

REIGNITE is your prescription for a balanced life.

The **REIGNITE** framework is a stepwise process designed for mitigating, alleviating, or eliminating the symptoms and causes of job-related burnout. Successfully completed, this process can transform an individual from burned out to ON FIRE with restoration of power, passion, and sense of purpose.

The steps in this process are simple. They will serve as a guide. The degree to which each of the steps will help you will be based entirely on the effort you put into each of them. Be committed to getting the utmost from working each of these steps.

As you go through each of the steps, be 100 percent willing to be transparent and authentic. This means becoming vulnerable. This will serve to ensure the best possible outcome for you from this training.

Faithfully finish all of the steps you are asked to complete. It will be worth your time and effort. In the end, I am confident you will get far more out of completing the exercises in this workbook than you anticipate.

As you work through **REIGNITE**, you will be asked to answer some questions. You can circle some responses and write others directly into this book. Or, you can download and print out a free REIGNITE Workbook for recording your answers. Get your free copy of the PDF file for the REIGNITE Workbook now at http://ReigniteBook. com/reignite-workbook/.

Here is an overview of the **REIGNITE** framework.

REIGNITE

REVIEW—your current circumstances and the events that have led to them.

ENVISION—your brightest preferred future.

INTROSPECTION—take an inventory of your core values and honestly assess the condition of all four of your life realms: mental, emotional, physical, and spiritual.

GENERATE—ideas and action plans to transform your life.

NEUTRALIZE—all of the self-placed obstacles and barriers.

IMPLEMENT—the plans you have made with a timetable of actionable steps with built-in accountability.

TRANSFORMATION—acknowledging and documenting your progression from feeling burned out to a new freedom and a new happiness.

ENGAGEMENT—celebrates a purpose-driven work life characterized by vigor, dedication, and absorption while experiencing a more authentic and joyous life overall.

Let's go through each of these one by one.

Review

Review your current circumstances and the events that have led to them. How did you get to where you are right now? Looking back, what do you see as the major decisions, turning points, or events that have led you to where you are right now in your career?

_____

_____

_____

_____

In life?

_____

_____

_____

_____

Do you feel your career has negatively impacted your personal life, or do you feel your personal life has negatively affected your career? How so?

_____

_____

_____

_____

Do you feel any of these circumstances are insurmountable? If so, which one(s)?

_____

_____

Is there one thing in particular over which you feel stuck?

_____

_____

Review the Hallmarks of Burnout

Which of the three hallmarks of JRB do you feel you have expressed?

- Emotional Exhaustion—A feeling of being emotionally depleted to the point where you feel you can no longer give of yourself at an emotional or psychological level to your company or the people you serve. KEYWORD: EXHAUSTION
- YES or NO
- Depersonalization—The development of negative and cynical feelings leading to a callous and dehumanized perception of patients, clients, or customers, which further leads to the view that they are somehow deserving of their problems and troubles. KEYWORD: CYNICISM
- YES or NO
- Lack of a Sense of Personal Accomplishment—You feel so little reward from what you do there is a tendency to evaluate yourself in negative terms, which leads to dissatisfaction and unhappiness in your work, creating a lack of a sense of personal accomplishment. KEYWORD: INEFFICACY
  YES or NO

Are you willing to change some things in order to alleviate or eliminate the symptoms of job-related burnout? YES or Not Yet

If not, what do you perceive are the barriers to making needed changes?

_____

_____

_____

_____

Review the Six Major Mismatches That Lead to JRB

Ninety percent of the time it is not the employees who burn themselves out; it is the work environment that burns out the employees. Here are six major mismatches between the job and the employee that lead to job-related burnout (JRB).

1. Work Overload
2. Lack of Control
3. Insufficient Reward
4. Breakdown of Community
5. Absence of Fairness
6. Conflicting Values

Many of the steps necessary to mitigate or alleviate the six major mismatches that cause job burnout require changes at the business's organizational level. These are most easily accomplished in small businesses.

If you are an employee of a large organization, changing the culture, management, and work environment of your employer may seem daunting or even impossible.

Nothing is impossible. It isn't about making your employer change. It is about leading them to a place where they want to make a change, a place where they feel that the proposed changes will benefit them.

You can show them how eliminating or preventing job-related burnout will:

- Decrease employee turnover and improve retention of needed talent
- Increase employee satisfaction and decrease employee complaints
- Decrease employee absenteeism
- Improve customer satisfaction and decrease customer complaints
- Increase the quality of products and services
- Eliminate work hostility and promote workplace harmony
- Decrease the threat of do-overs/recalls/lawsuits

Bottom-Bottom Line: Decreased costs and increased profit margins. What employer wouldn't be thrilled with this outcome?

Major Job Mismatches Self-Assessment

Which of the six major job-employee mismatches do you feel exist in your current work environment? Check all that apply. Then, for the ones you have checked, jot down one to three changes you would like to see occur that would mitigate or alleviate them. Go further by making some proposals as to how those changes might be accomplished. Be as specific as you can be. Finally, make a commitment as to which of the proposals you will personally make attempts to see enacted in your workplace.

Work Overload—Downsizing, budget cuts, layoffs, and reorganization efforts all usually result in three things: more work intensity, more demands on time, more job complexity. In short, people are required to do ever more with less. This can leave individuals exhausted.

Needed Changes:

_____

_____

Change Proposals:

_____

_____

Commitment:

_____

_____

Lack of Control—Organizations that become intolerant of creative problem solving in lieu of centralized control will squelch individual autonomy. This reduces an employee's capacity to set limits, exercise problem solving, select individualized approaches to work, allocate resources, and set priorities. The overall effect is a loss of interest in the job and monumental frustration.

Needed Changes:

_____

_____

Change Proposals:

_____

_____

Commitment:

_____

_____

Insufficient Reward—Market forces focusing on reducing costs have also reduced organizations' capacities to reward their employees in meaningful ways. People seek intangible rewards from meaningful work, such as money, security, recognition, benefits, intrinsic satisfaction, etc. If these are lacking, people naturally begin to wonder why they are working so hard. More work + less reward = dissatisfaction.

Needed Changes:

_____

_____

Change Proposals:

_____

_____

Commitment:

_____

_____

Breakdown of Community—As organizations grow larger or too quickly, a breakdown in the character of the organization can result as short-term profit is chased at the expense of interpersonal relationships within the company. This will inevitably lead to greater conflicts among employees, a lack of mutual support, lack of respect, and a growing sense of isolation. Dr. Maslach states, "A sense of belonging disappears when people work separately instead of together."

Needed Changes:

_____

_____

Change Proposals:

_____

_____

Commitment:

_____

_____

Absence of Fairness—Dr. Maslach perceives a workplace to be fair when three key elements are provided: trust, openness, and respect. When all three are present, employees are valued and they will in turn feel valued and remain fully engaged (the opposite of burnout). When these elements are absent, burnout will be the direct end result.

Needed Changes:

_____

_____

Change Proposals:

_____

_____

Commitment:

_____

_____

Conflicting Values—If organizations say they are dedicated to excellence yet take actions which damage the quality of the services or products they provide, then conflict results. This can be extremely frustrating and demoralizing to the employee, especially if their internal moral compass or core values are being assailed. To achieve a quality product or service, a company's values must remain in alignment with those of the employees.

Needed Changes:

_____

_____

Change Proposals:

_____

_____

Commitment:

_____

_____

*Do you feel these are present in your workplace?

TRUST? YES or NO
OPENNESS? YES or NO
RESPECT? YES or NO

Envision

Envision your brightest preferred future.

In this step you will envision your most desirable future life, living location, activities, relationships, living conditions, travel destinations, and health status. In other words, I want you to envision what your life will look like one, three, or five years from now. It will be a picture of your preferred future.

You should know your preferred future is your dream and no one else's. Translating your life from where you are to your preferred future is your job. No one else will do this for you because they are concerned about their own lives and their own preferred futures.

It is time to cast aside your life of variations in sameness. It is time to choose for yourself a life without self-imposed limitations. On the next few pages you will begin to write down what your preferred future will look like. Not just your professional life but your family life as well. All four of your personal life realms will be included too.

Your entries won't just be ethereal, someday hopes and dreams, or pie-in-the-sky aspirations. They will serve as concrete goals, which you will work toward one step at a time, always asking yourself, "So, what's the next step?" until your goals are reached.

Remember, no holding back. No self-imposed limitations.

Your imagination can make you infinite.

> "If you can imagine it, you can achieve it.
> If you can dream it, you can become it."
> **~ William Arthur Ward**

MY PREFERRED FUTURE

Describe what your ideal workday will look like. How many days per week would you work? How many hours per day? Would you work full time? Part-time? Would you work solo, or with a group of people? For an employer, or for yourself? How much vacation time would you have, and how often? Provide as much detail as you can.

_____

_____

_____

_____

Where would you work if you could work anywhere your heart desired? Would you stay where you are now, or would you want to work someplace different, doing something different?

Where are you living? What kind of dwelling would you call home? What would your family life look like? What is your debt situation?_____

Are you working, playing, or have you blended both so much an onlooker can't tell the difference? Are you a volunteer? A philanthropist? How will you be benefiting others? Who are you serving, and how?

What emotional issues will you have finally dealt with as you enter your preferred future?

Describe your preferred health status. What healthy goals will you have achieved?

What outside interests, hobbies, and activities are you enjoying in your future? What will you be doing to expand your interests outside of your work?

_____

_____

_____

_____

What will your spiritual life look like? What changes will you have made?

_____

_____

_____

_____

It is important to write these down completely with attention to detail. To end up precisely where you wish to be, you must have some sense of where you are headed.

> *"If you do not change direction,*
> *you may end up where you are heading."*
> **~ Lao Tzu**

I want you to be massively successful in whatever capacity you choose. The reason is simple. It will be much easier for you to give of yourself from a cup which is overflowing than from one which is never full or is almost always empty.

I want you to be able to serve and contribute to your passions, your work, your family, your community, and to the world from a position of abundance rather than struggle from a position of scarcity. It begins first by caring for yourself, perhaps in ways you never have before.

Completing this step will produce a roadmap you will use to get you to your desired destination. This is a very important part of your **REIG-NITE** journey.

Introspection

Introspection means taking inventory of your core values and honestly assessing the condition of all four of your life realms—mental, emotional, physical, and spiritual.

> If you have already completed a Core Values Inventory (CVI), then you already know your top five core values and your #1 core value. If you have not yet completed the CVI, do so as soon as possible. Go to http://ReigniteBook.com/the-core-values-inventory/ to download a FREE CVI which you can print out and complete at your earliest convenience.

The CVI is a process of self-discovery! Everyone has a set of core values that are integral to who they are or even to whom they profess to be. Your core values may change throughout the different seasons of your life, but they are always with you. When you form an opinion, make decisions, or make judgments, you are either honoring or dishonoring your core values in the process.

If you are honoring your core values, you are more likely to be happy. If you are dishonoring your core values, you are more likely to be miserable. Violating your own core values will lead to burnout at your job, in your personal life, and in living.

To be a person of honor is to possess and display integrity in one's beliefs and actions. This is most easily accomplished through one's core values. This is why everyone should take a Core Values Inventory.

Knowing your core values will offer crystal clear insight as to who you are. This, then, could be, should be used as a guide when making both the large and small decisions affecting your life.

We all make choices. All of us will experience consequences as a result of our choosing. If we choose poorly for ourselves, the consequences are likely to be undesirable. Alternatively, choosing based on a true reflection of who we are will help to ensure more positive outcomes.

Core-value-guided decision making helps immensely when choosing a career, a particular job, a mate, friends, associations, even a home or a car. Deciding in this way, in favor of your own core values, promotes synergy between you and the life you choose to live, and synergy promotes harmony.

Everyone has been confronted at some point in their life with a situation, decision, or request from someone that dishonors or goes against their inner compass or core values. Think back in your own life to whenever this has occurred. You probably said or thought something like: "I can't do that," or "This is not me," or "That's not who I am."

If you decided in your own favor, then you were honoring the core values that were being challenged. Afterward, you probably felt good about your decision. If you went counter to what you were telling yourself at the time and made the decision to proceed against your better judgment, then I am 100 percent certain you dishonored one or more of your core values.

Afterward, you probably felt bad about your decision. What was the ultimate outcome? How did decisions dishonoring your core values affect your life, positively or negatively? Conflicting values is one of the biggest of the six major mismatches between the job and the employee that creates burnout.

When you look back at the decisions you have made that brought you to where you are now, were those decisions dishonoring your core values?

If so, which decisions?

_____

_____

_____

_____

Deciding counter to our core values can lead to lying, cheating, stealing, burnout, bankruptcy, relationship problems, and all of the attendant negative consequences. Laboring in a career or at a particular job that violates our core values will ultimately lead to burnout. Burnout reflects immense personal dissatisfaction and unhappiness.

Self-inflicted or job-related burnout is no state in which to live. It is impossible to live a life of purpose and passion when burned out. The best way to avoid burnout is to celebrate and honor your own core values in everything you do and in every decision you make. When you are getting ready to make a decision, large or small, consider first whether or not the decision or potential outcome is in line with your core values. Determining your top five core values and your #1 main core value can be challenging but very enlightening; the process of self-discovery can even be enjoyable.

Your Mental Realm

Most professionals are very good at feeding their mental realms within the scope of their work. How about outside of work? For many, not so much.

Most professions encompass incomprehensibly large databases. No human could possibly know or learn all there is to know about a given profession, or in a single branch of profession for that matter.

No human can keep up with all of the new information being published every single day. Yet this does not prevent many from trying. Thank goodness that anything you want or need to know is easily accessible nowadays.

For too many, the thirst for knowledge begins and ends within their chosen profession. It's a shame, really. There is so much more out there to know and enjoy about life. Too many have stopped being curious about the world. Too many miss the benefits of learning outside their chosen fields. There are tangible benefits for doing so.

For instance, reading about bee and ant colonies can help you run and organize an office. Science fiction not only stimulates the imagination but predicts the future. Books on art and philosophy can give you insight into the human condition and why understanding behavior helps make your life and the lives of those around you better, more so than a whole bag of pills. I once read a book on quantum electrodynamics, specifically about particle entanglement, which made me realize just how interconnected we are, with everything! On top of all of that, these and other non-medical topics are just plain interesting, if you're curious. Curiosity, exploring, and learning should never stop with earning a degree, or be confined by it. If you aren't naturally curious, you can become curious with intention. It is a learned behavior.

Expand your knowledge base outside of work, and you will expand your horizons. Here are the fundamental steps needed for addressing the obstacles, challenges, shortcomings, or barriers to **REIGNITE** your mind.

Stimulate and nourish your brain. These are one and the same.

First, unless you are watching something purely educational, turn off the television. Most of what is on TV is crap and will make you stupid. If you must watch something for mindless entertainment, keep it under an hour a day. But just remember—they don't call it mindless entertainment for nothing.

Second, I can't think of anything that will get your mind stimulated faster than reading great books! Pick an area of interest outside of your work and read to find out what you don't know. You won't even know what you don't know, or what you need to know, until you start reading.

Author and career coach Dan Miller (*48 Days to the Work You Love*) suggests reading inspirational and uplifting books for at least 30 minutes each day. This is the best way I know to switch your brain to REIGNITE style thinking. This is something I do and wholeheartedly endorse.

Read non-work-related periodicals, as well, to stimulate your thinking. Foster a hobby. Read poetry and awesome quotes.

Listen to a variety of music and podcasts that interest you. There is nothing of interest you can't find on the internet. I have made this bet countless times with friends. I always win. The world is at your fingertips through the world wide web.

Are you stimulating and feeding your mind daily? If not, why not? What are the barriers to learning that you perceive? Are they real or imagined? Answer here.

_____

_____

_____

_____

Do you read and explore for learning purposes outside the discipline of your profession on a regular basis? YES or NO

If yes, what? _____

What do you wish you knew more about or had more time to learn outside of your profession?

_____

_____

_____

_____

Write down something you will commit to reading for learning outside of your profession on a regular basis.
Commitment:

_____

_____

_____

_____

Do you read for pure pleasure? YES or NO

What did you last read for pleasure and when?

_____

_____

_____

_____

If no, or more than one year ago, what will be your commitment for pleasure reading?

Commitment:

_____

_____

_____

_____

Your Emotional Realm

This is the second-most ignored realm. Personal emotional health, and how to foster it, is just not something to which a lot of time is devoted while growing up or within the educational system. Yet it is the realm which takes the heaviest toll when people burn out. The reason is simple: mental anguish is often worse than physical pain.

Emotional exhaustion is one of the hallmarks of JRB. It is the first hallmark women usually feel and the second hallmark men feel. It occurs when the individual can no longer give of himself/ herself to the client, customer, or patient on an emotional or psychological level. In essence, the person becomes emotionally spent or drained.

If the State of Happiness is a healthy mind, body, and spirit, then the capital city would be Emotional Wellbeing. If your emotional well-being is suffering, then chances are your mental, spiritual, and physical realms are suffering too. How does one repair damaged emotional wellbeing? What kind of transformation does that take? None of us are born emotionally damaged, ill, or bankrupt, yet this will be how some of us end up. People can feel beaten up emotionally by others, by circumstance, by lack of success, by life, and, of course, by burnout.

Some people display tremendous hardiness and are resilient. They overcome emotional setbacks without long-lasting impact. They may even thrive after an emotional setback.

Others languish and may break down mentally, physically, and spiritually because of uninterrupted emotional turmoil. Seemingly unable to turn things around, they can become paralyzed by their emotional misery.

When you are viewing everything through a corrupted and broken emotional lens, everything around you looks corrupted and broken too.

In the worst instances of emotional trauma, professional assistance may be necessary. If that sounds like you, seek professional help as quickly as possible. Know this: under the right circumstances and with proper care, everyone can heal emotionally.

But what is the difference between these two types of people, the ones who seem to turn things around for themselves under the worst possible circumstances and the people who seemingly can't? A twelve-year landmark study by a leading psychologist, Dr. Salvatore R. Maddi, found that those who thrived in spite of ruinous emotional stress possessed three key beliefs or traits that helped them weather adversity and turn it to their advantage.

It all came down to attitude: the commitment attitude that would lead them to act to be involved in ongoing events, the control attitude that would lead them to struggle to try and influence outcomes, and the challenge attitude that would lead them to view stressors, whether positive or negative, as new learning and growth opportunities. Dr. Maddi termed this hardiness. Others refer to it as resilience.

The operative word here is attitude. I like the word mindset. Is your mindset something that is handed to you by someone else, dictated by circumstance, or something you are born with, perhaps? No, like so much else in life, the mindset you have about anything and everything is a personal choice.

Good emotional health doesn't automatically fall onto you from the sky as you sit and contemplate all that is wrong with your life. Emotional balance is something that can be cultivated and developed. Like anything else in life that is worthwhile, it takes choosing differently for yourself, some effort, some practice, some patience, and time.

Some might argue that this is easy to do for people who are successful. They conclude it is easier to be happy, hardy, and more resilient when you're successful. Right? In reality, the exact opposite is true.

Psychologist Dr. Sonja Lyubomirsky of the University of California, Riverside found that chronically happy people turn out to be more successful across many life domains than people that are less happy. Makes sense. The surprise was that their happiness was in large part a direct consequence of their positive emotions and attitudes rather than their success.

The people he studied were happy before they were successful. They became more successful because they were happy. Here it is in a nutshell:

HAPPINESS = SUCCESS = HAPPINESS

It is time to state something clearly and unequivocally here. Everyone is entitled to their own emotions. Everyone should own their own emotions and be wholly responsible for them. It is then, and only then, that one is able to change them.

How do you make yourself happy? Well, I know how to do that for myself. I have no idea how to make you happy. That is your journey. I do have a general sense of what it might take to make happiness easier to obtain for most people who aren't happy.

Embrace, cling to, devour the positive aspects of living. Read poetry, uplifting books, inspirational stories. Improve yourself. Learn! Watch comedies. Laugh! Laugh some more. Laugh at yourself.

Avoid negativity. Norman Vincent Peale once said, "Avoid like the plague those who fail to crystallize you to your full potential." He is saying avoid negative people as you would a suppurative, plague-induced, cyst-draining pus. That's pretty emphatic.

Surround yourself with positive people. Decide to become, at all costs, a positive person. It is but a choice after all.

A positive Transformation requires positive input. Negativity is anathema to positive change. No one would begin a race while tethered to the ground.

Negative attitudes, beliefs, outlooks, forecasting, viewpoints, approaches, and positions are just binders that keep us stuck. Whether they come from within or from outside ourselves makes no difference.

Make this pledge to yourself:

"I am going to become a more positive person by surrounding myself with positive and uplifting people, exploring and employing resources for positive thinking and behaviors, while avoiding negativity like the plague."

Avoid negativity like the plague because it will poison the wellspring of your soul. This must begin within yourself first. This may take some getting used to if you have trained your brain to think or react negatively to any given situation.

Like any bad behavior that has been learned, negative thinking can be un-learned. It doesn't just happen by trying to think positively all of the time. It comes from learning to think positively, and that means being proactive. Here are three steps to help you accomplish this.

1. Begin to read positive, uplifting, inspiring, challenging, and affirming material. In whatever your area of interest, find great books and read them! Go to the websites of people you admire and search their reading lists. Most will have one, and you will begin to notice the wells from which they draw their experience, strength, and hope. Study their sources of inspiration.

2. If you live your life according to what is presented in the popular press, we are supposed to be afraid of something, in dire need of something, or imminently dying from something 24/7. Mainstream news is all about what is deficient, broken, or missing. If there is an occasional feel-good story, it is always used as a hook to get you to watch the gloom and doom forecast and reporting.

3. The internet has greatly expanded our news source horizons. Look for blogs, websites, and podcasts full of positive information that will help inspire, motivate, and crystallize you to your full potential. Everything else is a distraction and a waste of your time.

4. Surround yourself with like-minded, purpose-driven, passionate people. Avoid negative individuals wherever possible or at least learn how to filter out their negativity. If someone offers you a neg-

ative sentiment or observation, don't waste energy disagreeing with it. Rather, try to rev up your positivity generator by countering their statement with a positive spin or comment.

5. Challenge and then change your mindset. Look for the positive in everything. Notice positive occurrences throughout your day and begin to comment on them out loud to others.

6. Are you a positive person? Try to go an entire day without making negative or derogatory statements. This does not mean that you are to stop giving or receiving constructive criticism. Honest constructive criticism is positive, good, and helpful, not at all negative. You know the difference. What additional steps can you think of to increase and accentuate the positive in your life?

These steps and others will help you to regain control over any pessimism and cynicism that may be dogging you. Or, maybe your positive-mindset generator is just in need of a tune-up rather than an overhaul. Either way, taking ownership of this step of your Transformation is sure to brighten your pathway to the future you wish to create for yourself.

How many hours per day do you watch television? _____

Commitment:_____max.

How much time per day do you spend on meditation, prayer, or quiet time?

_____

_____

Commitment: *(20–30 minutes minimum recommended)*

_____

_____

How many hours or minutes per day do you spend reading or listening to motivational and inspirational content?

_____

_____

Commitment:

_____

_____

Thinking about the people you hang out with most often, would you describe them as more (circle one) NEGATIVE NEUTRAL POSITIVE?

Are you a (or the) negative voice in a group setting? YES or NO
If yes, how could you change this?

_____

_____

Do you have a colleague(s) who you confide in often? YES or NO If no, will you commit to finding someone with whom you trust? List three possibilities:

_____

_____

How do you get your news?

_____

_____

Do you feel BETTER or WORSE (circle one) about the world after listening to the news? If worse, what would be a solution for this?

_____

_____

Do you keep a journal?
YES or NO If no, would this be beneficial for you?

YES or NO If yes, what will be your commitment for journaling? Commitment:

_____

_____

Are you hardy, resilient, and happy, or emotionally unbalanced? Are you thriving, or in need of emotional transformation?

_____

_____

Your Physical Realm

As physically conditioned as they are, athletes know their game is mostly mental. As a nation of mostly out-of-shape people, the mental energy required to begin a regular program of exercise and to maintain it to the point of achieving and perpetuating results can seem unconquerable.

There is a part of TRANSFORMATION that is often overlooked when most people begin to change their lives for the better and in profound ways: the physical realm. You will never be the best you can be, the best you can become, if your physical house isn't in order.

Completely transforming yourself and your life into the person you want to be, living the life you want to live, doing the kind of work you want to do is going to require some effort. Being physically fit will help you to accomplish the work that will be required to reach your goals. It's absolutely necessary, and it will make your transformation a whole lot easier and much more enjoyable.

To be more mentally fit, you must become more physically fit. You might ask, "What has one to do with the other?" I have never seen a mentally fit person who felt as mentally sharp as they were capable of feeling if they felt poorly in their body.

Similarly, I have never seen a physically fit person who felt well in their body if they were suffering mentally. We all live inside our heads. What and how we "feel" is a summation of our mental, emotional, spiritual, and our physical feelings.

The sense of wellbeing that we all seek is a balance between all four realms: the mental, emotional, physical, and spiritual. Care for three and ignore the one, and your life will be out of balance. In my profession, the physical realm is the one most often ignored by doctors. Go figure. We recommend regular cardiovascular exercise to our patients, but as a group doctors could do much better.

Trimming down, eating healthy, and exercising regularly will make you feel great, like you can conquer the world! You will have more energy, more stamina, get sick less often, and you'll live longer. If you can't manage to be totally fit, then be as fit as you can be.

Regular, heart-pumping exercise gives you a sense of calm and wellbeing that you cannot get from a pill or a pep talk. Exercise boosts the immune system, clears the mind, lifts the spirits, and alleviates depression and anxiety. In short, it enhances your other three realms. Improving your physical health will improve all of them without any additional effort.

If you are going to transform, then why not transform your physical status from unhealthy to healthy? It is never too late to start. Small changes add up and amplify over time.

Getting physically fit means getting your mindset right first. I was having a conversation recently with a friend over the tremendous influence of one's mindset. I gave him examples of how two totally different mindsets can lead to completely unexpected and disparate outcomes. The examples I used astonished my friend, and me. Until that moment, I had not fully realized the power potential of one's mindset.

Over the years, my work as a family physician has afforded me the opportunity to interact with all types of patients with all sorts of medical problems and all manner of emotional difficulties. Never is my job made more difficult than when dealing with a patient's fixed, unyielding, rigid mindset.

It seems that once a person locks into a certain paradigm in their way of thinking, which then dictates a certain patterned behavior, it becomes extremely difficult to change their mindset, even if their mindset is harmful to them. This is especially difficult if their behavior has been enabled, supported, or provides other secondary gain.

Here are some cases in point. Over my practice career, I have cared for two completely unrelated paraplegic patients. Each was paralyzed from the waist down. Each were bound to their wheelchairs when up and about. Each had their cars equipped for driving. Each of them had full-time jobs.

Each of them always came to my office unaccompanied for their appointments. They would retrieve, set up, use, and then return their wheelchairs from behind the driver's seat of their automobiles all by themselves.

They had families but rarely asked for their help. They valued their independence and did not wish to be considered handicapped. And they never, never asked me for a handicapped placard for their cars.

In stark contrast, at least once every week or two, I'd have patients with back pain, knee pain, hip pain, morbid obesity, or patients just pitifully out of shape ask me for handicapped placards for their cars. These were individuals who would walk into my office under their own power without any assistance from others or without assistance devices such as canes or walkers. In other words, most of them were able-bodied.

Here are the criteria set by the state of North Carolina as qualifications for a handicapped vehicular placard.
- Cannot walk 200 feet without stopping to rest.
- Cannot walk 200 feet without an assistance device.
- Is restricted by severe lung disease.
- Uses portable oxygen.
- Has a Class III or IV cardiac condition.
- Is severely limited in their ability to walk due to arthritic, neurological or orthopedic conditions.
- Is totally blind or eyesight is severely limited (shouldn't be driving anyway).

Most of the patients asking for handicapped placards do not meet any of these criteria. When I suggested they did not need one, that they should start parking as far away from the front door of the mall as possible, all were disappointed and more than a few became incensed. In my defense, it was my job to do what was best for them, even if they did not agree.

For those patients with back, hip, knee, or ankle/foot pain, most of the time the primary underlying cause was inactivity or obesity due to unhealthy eating and lack of adequate exercise. This is what was interesting about their request, were I to have granted. Even if they were able to park thirty, fifty, or eighty feet closer to the door front door of a business, they would walk much further once inside the doors of the stores.

The difference between those patients and the two paraplegic patients is the difference between night and day. The paraplegic patients with obvious physical disability did not wish to be considered handicapped, while the able-bodied patients wanted to be considered handicapped.

So, what's the fundamental difference? The paraplegic patients do not believe they were handicapped while the able-bodied patients believed they were. The difference, in a word, is MINDSET. Mindset is a powerful potential force. I say potential force because it is just as potent either way, for good or for ill. It can open people up to tremendous possibilities or lock others into a life of considerably less, even one of self-pronounced disability.

"Why?" you might ask. The answer doesn't come down to a question of genes, luck, intelligence, or resources. It comes down to a simple choice. With few exceptions, mindset can overcome physical, mental, and emotional disability.

I had a gentleman in his seventies who had a dense right-sided stroke which left him with a flaccid left arm and leg. He came into the office in a wheelchair six weeks after his stroke, unable to move any finger of his left hand, flex at the left wrist or elbow, raise his arm, bend any toe of his left foot, or stand without assistance, much less walk.

At his family's request, I filled out and signed a form for a handicapped placard to make it easier for him to be transported. He asked me if he would ever recover any use of his now-useless left side. Conventional wisdom is that whatever remains after six weeks is what will remain and whatever is lost will remain lost.

I have never been one to take away a patient's hope, and I have witnessed amazing recoveries. So, I looked him in the eye and told him it would be entirely up to him.

Most patients who get rehab will attempt the rehabilitation exercises only as long as they are with the physical therapist and then stop after they are gone. I told him he could rewire around the damaged areas of his brain if he made it his number one priority. It would be very hard and take time but, I thought it was entirely possible. He left my office determined.

When I saw him again a few months later, he was still in his wheelchair but he proudly demonstrated for me how he could flex ever so slightly two of the fingers of his left hand. He told me how he would sit all day concentrating and working on moving those two fingers.

Many months later, he presented with a very weak grip in his left hand. He was also able to flex slightly at the shoulder and bend his left great toe a bit. Months after that, he was able to shake my hand with a stronger grip while flexing some at the left elbow and shoulder. His family would tell me about how he would sit every day squeezing a tennis ball while listening to uplifting music, sun up to sundown.

Always positive, always smiling, I never saw him down or in a bad mood. He showed me something new he could do each time he came back in for a checkup. One day, a few years after his stroke event, he walked into my office pushing a walker wearing a brace on his left lower leg and foot which kept it at a 90-degree angle so he wouldn't trip.

He was able to raise his left arm to shoulder level, and he had dexterous use of his left hand. He reached into his pocket with his left hand to retrieve something he said he wanted to give me. He said, "I don't need this anymore." It was his handicapped placard.

He gave me a hug and thanked me for all I had done for him, at which point I was reduced to tears. What had I done for this man? I gave him a few simple words. He made a choice. He did all the work. He essentially moved a mountain all by himself. I made sure he knew it too.

Whatever I did for him pales in comparison to what he has done for me. He continues to serve as an inspiration to me, proof of what is possible with the proper mindset. He makes me grateful I went into medicine in the first place.

He continued to improve. It has been eight years since his stroke. He now walks into my office under his own power with no walker and no leg brace.

He has full and complete use of his left side. Anyone would be hard pressed to know he was once completely paralyzed on his left side just by watching him move. Now in his 80s, he drives himself to the Family Y every day, parks next to the street, and walks on in to work out.

All my able-bodied patients requesting handicapped placards have chosen a mindset powered by limitations, which to them, appear everywhere. My patient who recovered from stroke and the two paraplegic patients share something in common, too: in spite of physical disability, they each chose a mindset powered by potential, one without limitations… and for them, there were none.

Do you feel you have limitations? How is your mindset? Is it in need of revision?

You can achieve nearly any level of fitness you desire, even if you have physical limitations. If you are above the age of forty, have some health issues, or are unsure of your health status, then be sure to consult with your own physician first to see what kind of diet and exercise program is best and safest for you. If you already enjoy the best health you can have for your age, then you are one step ahead on your way to **REIGNITE**.

Do you have a physician you see regularly? YES or NO
If no, enter a date by which time you will have obtained one.
Commitment:

_____

_____

Personal physician candidates:

_____

_____

If yes, do you follow your physician's instructions? YES or NO Remember, your doctor is your healthcare consultant. It serves no purpose to hire a professional consultant only to ignore their prudent advice.

Do you get regular checkups? YES or NO
If no, enter a date by which you will have obtained a complete checkup.
Commitment:

_____

_____

Are you up to date on all of your health screening and health maintenance measures? YES or NO If no, enter a date by which you will be.
Commitment:

_____

_____

Do you do some type of regular cardiovascular exercise? YES or NO
If yes, what? (Claiming yard work, house work, or a round of golf as cardiovascular exercise is like claiming you got useful information from a book you never read but just happened to walk past.)

_____

_____

If no, write down one form of cardiovascular exercise you will commit to doing regularly beginning ASAP (pending clearance from your doctor).
Commitment:

_____

_____

Do you hike, run, or do water sports, or something else out-of- doors regularly? YES or NO
If yes, what?

_____

_____

If no, write down one outside activity you will commit to regularly.
Commitment:

_____

_____

Do you get adequate rest? YES or NO
How many hours of sleep do you get each night on average? Commitment:
(minimum 7½ hours average is recommended)

_____

_____

Do you feel you need to lose weight? YES or NO
If yes, what realistic amount will you commit to losing over the next one
year with a proper diet and exercise program?
Commitment:

_____

_____

Have you been wanting to join a gym for exercise? YES or NO
If yes, enter a date by which time you will have joined a gym.

Commitment:

_____

_____

Other ways you might improve your physical realm:

_____

_____

_____

Your Spiritual Realm

No self-help assessment or effort can be complete unless you address the health of your spiritual self. If you are to **REIGNITE** your life, not just change it, then your spiritual realm is just as important as the other three realms. Maybe even more so. It is the deepest part of you.

The spirit encompasses your sense of who you are, why you are here, and your place in the world. It represents your connectedness, or lack of connectedness, to other people, to nature, and reality. Your spiritual health is reflected in your sense of purpose. Do you know with certainty what you stand for? Have you developed a manifesto on life or a philosophy for living? Do you know why you are here? If not, are you still searching?

So, how is your spiritual health? Do you feel connected to humanity, a higher power, nature, and the world around you? Do you have hope for the future, face each day with excitement, and feel optimistic, a sense of peace, a sense of calm, and serenity? If so, you are in excellent spiritual health.

Or, do you live in fear under a prevailing sense of dread, feel you walk alone in this world, prefer pessimism over optimism, feel hopeless or helpless, feel empty or apathetic and anxious for the future? Do you have unnamed or unreasonable fears? Do you feel you know who you are and have a sense of purpose? Or, are you somewhere in between these two extremes? If so, then your spiritual self may be damaged or suffering.

When I was an active alcoholic, my spiritual health was very poor. I felt dead inside. I felt it was impossible to change my circumstances, which gave me no hope for the future. I heard someone once describe how they felt when they hit their rocky bottom with drug addiction. He said he felt "perfectly broken."

That is precisely how I felt, perfectly broken. Many of you may feel this way if you are instead "perfectly burned out."

There are many opportunities that can enhance a damaged spirit or restore a broken one.

Be quiet and meditate every day. Concentrate on the things that you do have rather than dwell on what you don't have or feel you must have in order to be happy. Be grateful.

Avoid neediness. There is abundance everywhere you look. If you have a scarcity mindset, as if there isn't enough to go around, this should be a signal your spiritual realm needs some attention. Neediness is a form of self-rejection. We self-reject when we feel incomplete spiritually.

Get adequate rest! Play! Adults need to play just like children. Find ways to reconnect with your inner child. Color with crayons (especially outside the lines), draw, play with play mud, run with scissors (okay, blunt ones), get in a tickle fight.

Sounds silly, I know. That's the point. Silly makes people laugh. Silly makes people smile. When you laugh and smile, you feel happy. It lifts your spirit.

You want to feel younger in less than five seconds or less? Get up out of your chair right now and skip! It will immediately make you smile or laugh. That is your inner child laughing. The spirit of a child is boundless and free. Your child-self is still inside you. It wants you to come out and play. Don't say, "Maybe later."

Practice mindfulness. If there is something that you really enjoy, then really enjoy it. Slow down and savor everything worthy of your time and attention. Practice kindness, patience, the art of grace, empathy, and compassion. Be decent and tolerant. Be honest. Tell the truth.

Study art. Start with what you like, and then branch out. Take an art class. If you say that you aren't artistic and are of the opinion that artists are born, I will tell you that you are wrong. If artists are born, then there are just over seven billion of them on the planet and you are one of them. Take an art class and prove me wrong.

Listen to uplifting music. Again, start with what you like or are familiar with and branch out from there. If you can make music, then make it, and then make some more. Make music with others. Make music for others.

Connect with other people. Become part of a community. Well, except the, "Blah, blah, blah, nobody loves me; everybody hates me," community. That one is off limits. Look around. There are so many different and interesting communities out there to which you can belong. Pick one that will capture your interest and keep you energized.

Connect with animals. Do you have a pet? Some of my most cherished memories are of my pets. There are powerful stories that connect people and their pets. Pets can bring out the best in people. They will teach us valuable lessons if we let them. Do you have stories about a beloved pet?

Laugh. Laugh again. Laugh some more, especially at yourself. Go to a comedy club. Watch some of the old comedy shows that made you laugh when you were younger. You can find them all on the internet these days. Carol Burnett, Harvey Korman, Tim Conway, and Vicki Lawrence still crack me up. If I am feeling sad, all I have to do is pull up a YouTube clip and I am laughing out loud in less than a minute.

Give of yourself to others. Give your time. Volunteer. Help those less fortunate. Open your heart. Open your mind. In all things, try to be positive. Avoid negativity like it will kill you because it will if you let it. Share your most powerful words and stories with others.

Lastly, love yourself. You are not some pitiful, worthless creature to be loathed and despised, deserving of the worst the world has to offer. You are a luminous being, a child of the Universe. My goodness, there is only one of you. There will never again be one of you. Laugh, love, live!

Do not deny yourself the wonders life in the world has to offer. You were born with a natural set of God-given talents and abilities, which will allow you to improve any circumstance if you will but choose to do so. You may have forgotten this, but I haven't. The people who love you haven't.

How is your spiritual health? POOR GOOD GREAT AWESOME
Do you consider yourself a spiritual person? If yes, how so?

If not, list three ways you could try to become more spiritual

_____
_____
_____
_____
_____

Do you feel connected to the world and people in it? YES or NO
If yes, GREAT! If no, list five things which you pledge to do which will foster that sense of interconnectedness.

_____

_____

_____

_____

Do you take real vacations? YES or NO
If no, I want you to plan a trip right now. I will go to_____
by _____(within the next five months) for one full week minimum.
I pledge absolutely no working or studying while on vacation.

Signed:_____ Date:_____

Do you volunteer your time to a cause you support? YES or NO
If not, is there one you could? _____

Do you go out into natural surroundings on a regular basis? If so, how?

_____

_____

_____

_____

_____

If not, list the kinds of outdoor activities which would interest you.

_____

_____

_____

_____

Do you go to museums? YES or NO
If yes, what kind, where and when was the last time?

_____

_____

_____

If not, if you were to pick one, where would it be and when?

_____

_____

_____

What is your commitment to visiting a museum in the future?
Commitment:

_____

_____

_____

Do you create art? YES or NO
If so, what kind?

_____

_____

_____

How often?

_____

If not, what would you be willing to try and when?

_____

_____

_____

Commitment:

_____

_____

Do you keep a journal? Would this be beneficial for your spiritual growth?
YES or NO
If yes, what will be your commitment for journaling?
Commitment:

_____

_____

_____

*"You are not a drop in the ocean.
You are the entire ocean, in a drop."*
~ Rumi

Generate
Generate ideas and action plans to TRANSFORM your life.

As you know, nothing stays the same, ever. But most people want things to stay the same forever. Why? Where does that come from when it is completely outside of the human experience? I don't know.

Change is inevitable. Since it is inevitable, I believe it is better to try and choose your changes rather than have change choose you. It is a matter of planning, being proactive and intentional in our actions.

It is always nice to have options or choices. They are branch points on the decision tree of life that allow us to exercise some measure of control over our destiny. Sometimes options are numerous and we can pick our direction leisurely and without a lot of attendant anxiety.

Sometimes, our options are severely limited and we are forced to make hard choices. We have all been in the undesirable position of having to "choose the lesser of two evils." You may be there now. But, wasn't it a series of options and choices that put us in such predicaments in first place?

Ideally, it would be best to have more options, better options most of the time, and fewer instances where options are wholly constrained in scope with only frighteningly dreadful choices remaining. In this section, you will begin to open up to the options which are available to you.

The first step of TRANSFORMING your life is not a physical one. It is a mental step. It requires a change of one's mindset, a transformation in one's thinking. Win, lose, or draw, that is where the hardest battles are fought—in the mind.

There is also a difference between change and transformation. You can change your hairstyle, your clothes, your car, where you live, your job, and your friends, but none of that will change you, who you are. When I talk about a transformation, I am talking about changes on the inside as well as on the outside.

Transformation isn't about becoming somebody different either. It is about becoming the more authentic version of you, living a life that is concert with your core being, fully utilizing all of your unique natural talents and abilities. It is a metamorphosis.

Transformational change means fully elaborating your true self and acting accordingly. It all begins with accepting the notion: "My life is not what I want it to be, and I feel the need to change."

If you are ready, we will begin to generate ideas and action plans to TRANSFORM your life which will take you from where you are into your preferred future.

In this step you will bring over the action items that are the most important to you from the MY PREFERRED FUTURE section, pages 90-91. You will begin to list them in templates on the next several pages. For each category you will list each item under Current Circumstance and your preferred future outcome under Desired Outcome.

The really important action takes place in between, under Next Steps. Here you will begin to list what it will take to get you from where you are to where you desire to be. Getting from any point A to any point B is a progressive series of steps.

At this point, you do not have to precisely know every single step needed to get you to your desired outcome. You may inadvertently leave out a necessary step which is unknown to you at this time or you might need to adjust some of the steps as you go. Start with the most obvious and basic step first. Then ask yourself, "What's the next step?" Then, "What's the next step?" and so on.

All of your focus and energy should be applied to writing out sequentially each needed step to reach your desired outcome. You can make adjustments as you go. Add new steps if needed. Never stop, though. Keep marching through them. Don't worry about filling in any start/stop dates just now. Those will be added later.

What a wonderful gift the universe has given us,
the ability to transform

Action Item Template EXAMPLES

Action Template Example #1

Background: Dr. I. R. Grumpy—I am a 54-year-old, male family physician, and I became completely burned out at my job after just 17 years in private practice. I came to feel emotionally spent and exhausted. I grew cynical, feeling I had nothing left to give to my patients, whom I began to resent much of the time. I felt as though nothing I did was making a difference anymore. I lived for the weekends and dreaded Mondays. Activities, hobbies, and even the practice of medicine no longer interested me. I became irritable and moody at home. My family life began to suffer. I contemplated leaving the medical profession altogether until I participated in a workshop on job-related burnout. After acquiring the tools I needed to overcome burnout, I formulated a plan to alleviate my symptoms, correct the underlying causes, and recapture the joy and pleasure of practicing medicine and a balanced life.

Professional Life—Physician, Family Medicine
Current Circumstance:_____Begin Date Feb. 15, 2009
Completely burned out at work, hate my job.

Next Steps:
- Cut down on work hours to three ten-hour days/week.
- Delegate non-medical responsibilities at work.
- Resign from all board seats not passionate about.
- Get off extra, non-mandatory hospital committees.
- Identify several colleagues for support.
- Reduce call responsibilities.
- Volunteer more time in a free clinic.
- Restrict certain patients/procedures I don't enjoy.
- Restrict number of patients seen per hour.

Desired Outcome

Enjoy medicine again. Have a better attitude/outlook/energy level. Achieve desired outcome by *May15, 2009.

* I was able to accomplish all of these goals within two weeks! The positive effects were immediate, profound, and lasting.

Action Template Example #2

Background: Jane I. Hatemyjob—I am a 37-year-old social worker, and I have come to despise my work life. When I started my career in social work, I was energized, idealistic, and passionate about my work. Now I feel as if I'm stretched too thin by what I do. I feel exhausted most of the time, even when I'm off from work. People gossip and argue incessantly at the office, and employee turnover is very high. My coworkers have nothing good to say about our organization, or each other. I feel unsupported, unappreciated, and expendable. Nothing I do during my day seems to make a difference anymore. I can never finish my work, yet more gets piled onto my desk every single day. Management is not at all sympathetic to my pleas for help or responsive to my suggestions for needed change. I have almost completely stopped caring for the very people I want to help, the people I choose to help. Even my outlook on life in general has soured.

At the same time, I feel guilty for the way I am feeling. I'm left wondering, is this all there is?

Professional Life—Social Worker

Current Circumstance_____Begin Date_____

I feel burned out and unfulfilled, but I'm afraid to change. Social work is all I know; it's all I ever wanted to do. I want more out of life than the way I'm currently feeling.

Next Steps:

- Realize my current work situation is toxic and not likely to change.
- Acknowledge I am good at what I do and confirm it is still what I want to do.
- Accept if I do not like my current circumstances and know that I can change them.
- Know that all I want out of life I must change them.
- Know that there is an employer out there that will appreciate my expertise.
- Know that there is an employer out there who will appreciate my work ethic.
- Revise and punch up my professional resume. Begin a job search for organizations that will be a better fit for me.
- Send out three resumes and emails and make three follow-up calls every day.
- Know I am well equipped and adaptable for any job in my field.
- I pledge to be consistent and persistent until I get the job I desire.

Desired Outcome:

I will obtain a social work position with a for-profit or nonprofit organization that will appreciate me and allow me to utilize my talents and abilities to the fullest extent possible. This new employer will challenge me but offer tangible rewards for above-and-beyond efforts and provide opportunities for advancement.

Achieve desired outcome by _____

Action Template Example #3

Background: Tom A. Smoldering—I am a 47-year-old financial officer, and I feel dead inside. After 23 years of dedicated work for my company, I no longer feel any reward from my job. In fact, I have come to hate my job. I can't wait for Fridays, and the thought of going to work on Mondays makes me nauseous. What I do isn't particularly difficult, using my available skill sets, but that's just it. There is no challenge to my job anymore. I just do as I'm told. There is no room for innovation or creativity, and I feel isolated in my cubicle. Sometimes I feel like a robot could do my job. I have a long commute and work long hours. I hardly see my family, except on weekends. The most reward I get in the arena of finance is the work I do on the side with private clients. All of their situations are different, and some are quite complicated. I feel great satisfaction in being able to help and guide them. More and more people are asking me to work with them. Although I have 23 years with my company, the thought of putting my head down and grinding away at my current job for another 18 years makes me want to throw up. I have toyed with the idea of starting my own business.

Professional Life— Financial Officer, Private Finance Coach

Current Circumstance:_____ Begin Date _____

I hate my job but not necessarily my work. I am stressing over a decision to stay with my company and tough it out or start my own business.

Next Steps:
- Identify the barriers I feel I have toward starting my own business.
- Ascertain if these are real barriers or imagined barriers.
- Remove any real barriers and set aside the imagined ones.
- Identify the area of finance that appeals to me most.
- Invest in myself by picking up any tools I may be missing.

- Clearly define my ideal client.
- Accept that change may be hard but often the best option.
- Begin to market my services to my ideal clients.
- What I don't know about marketing, I will learn.
- When I am earning at least two thirds of my income from side work, I will quit my company job and continue to build my own business.
- Hire a business coach to help stay me on track and accountable.

Desired Outcome:

I will create a thriving finance consulting business, working with both individual clients and small business owners. I will set my own hours and work as hard or as little as I wish. I will learn new skills and continue to stretch in new and exciting directions. With plenty of income and flexible hours, I will spend much more quality time with my family.

Achieve desired outcome by _____

Professional Life

Current Circumstance:

_____

_____

_____

Next Steps

_____

_____

_____

Desired Outcome:

_____

_____

_____

Family Life—
Current Circumstance:

_____

_____

_____

Next Steps

_____

_____

_____

Desired Outcome:

_____

_____

_____

Mental Realm
Current Circumstance:

_____

_____

_____

Next Steps

_____

_____

_____

Desired Outcome:

_____

_____

_____

Emotional Realm
Current Circumstance:

_____

_____

_____

Next Steps

_____

_____

_____

Desired Outcome:

_____

_____

_____

Physical Realm
Current Circumstance:

_____

_____

_____

Next Steps

_____

_____

_____

Desired Outcome:

_____

_____

_____

Spiritual Realm
Current Circumstance:

_____

_____

_____

Next Steps

_____

_____

_____

Desired Outcome:

_____

_____

_____

Personal Debt
Current Circumstance:

_____

_____

_____

Next Steps

_____

_____

_____

Desired Outcome:

_____

_____

_____

Social Arena—

Current Circumstance:

_____

_____

_____

Next Steps

_____

_____

_____

Desired Outcome:

_____

_____

_____

_____ **(Fill your own targeted heading in the blank.)**

Current Circumstance:

_____

_____

_____

Next Steps

_____

_____

_____

Desired Outcome:

_____

_____

_____

_____ **(Fill your own targeted heading in the blank.)**

Current Circumstance:

_____

_____

_____

Next Steps

_____

_____

_____

Desired Outcome:

_____

_____

_____

_____ **(Fill your own targeted heading in the blank.)**

Current Circumstance:

_____

_____

_____

Next Steps

_____

_____

_____

Desired Outcome:

_____

_____

_____

_____ **(Fill your own targeted heading in the blank.)**

Current Circumstance:

_____

_____

_____

Next Steps

_____

_____

_____

Desired Outcome:

_____

_____

_____

_____ **(Fill your own targeted heading in the blank.)**

Current Circumstance:

_____

_____

_____

Next Steps

_____

_____

_____

Desired Outcome:

_____

_____

_____

_____ **(Fill your own targeted heading in the blank.)**
Current Circumstance:

_____

_____

_____

Next Steps

_____

_____

_____

Desired Outcome:

_____

_____

_____

Neutralize

One day, in continuous misery and feeling totally defeated, I had an epiphany. I came to realize I had no place left to go, but everywhere. I had no one left to see, but everyone. I had nothing left to do, but everything.

Neutralize all of the self-placed obstacles and barriers.

> *"And the day came when the risk to remain*
> *tight in a bud was more painful than the risk*
> *it took to blossom."*
> **~ Anais Nin**

> *"My dear friend, clear your mind of can't."*
> **~ Samuel Johnson**

No matter what new idea, notion, invention, innovation, product, service, business idea, or change you might be considering, the first voice you will hear, the loudest voice you will hear, sometimes the only voice you will hear saying **STOP** or **NO**, will be your own. Even now, this inner voice is saying things to you like: "You can't," "You shouldn't," "It's impossible," "You're an imposter," "You're going to fail," "It's too late," or "You don't know what you're doing."

If you say "I can't," I will not believe you, even though you will be right 100 percent of the time. My not believing that it is true will not make any difference, though, until you stop believing that it is true, at which point you will again be right 100 percent of the time. It is the only instance in your life when you will be 100 percent right either way. Your choice.

The words "I can't," or "That's impossible," form very finite statements. What would be, could be, and should be begins and ends with those words. After those words, there is nothing left to add. They are declarations of cessation, of complete arrest and of conclusion. They are a barricade to further effort. The end.

Negative notions like "I can't," or "That's impossible," are powerful words. They hold people back and down of their own volition. They are dream-stoppers and hope-enders. The mere utterance of these words destroys initiative, stifles creativity, and limits growth. They do not even have to be spoken in order to feel their full force. Just thinking these words is enough. How powerful is that?

For most people insisting on employing the "I can't" mentality, let's just get it right from the outset and translate this to what it actually means: "I won't." That might sound harsh, but it's the truth. The truth only sounds harsh because it's the truth.

If you are full of discontent, unhappiness, and discomfiture and are looking for a sign for when to begin to transform your life, your sign is discontent, unhappiness, and discomfiture.

Do you often hear yourself say "I can't?" Was it last week? Yesterday? Perhaps today? Doesn't it shut you down cold? The only meaning to extract from "I can't," is "I am unable."

Saying "I can," means you are able to do something. This increases the potential that you **will** do something. Saying "I can," and taking action means no matter what the outcome, you have already won a different future for yourself.

What about the impossible? To say "I can imagine that's possible," would be the most likely opposing viewpoint. What I want to know is why some feel compelled to cry "impossible," before fully exploring what can be imagined to be possible?

The brain is an amazing organ. What it is unable to do, it can imagine doing. What can be imagined creates possibilities. Possibilities have a habit of turning into reality with time and effort. Which makes me wonder, exactly what cannot be accomplished? I mean, really?

Looking back, wouldn't you agree that much of what once seemed impossible is now not only possible but a reality? It's because someone dared to rethink the impossible.

If you have a goal in mind, is it the best one for you, or have you compromised? Have you thought of other better goals but rejected them because you felt they were too difficult or impossible? Why? Why do we limit ourselves so?

Look around. Those happy and successful people around you who made plans for brightening their own futures while brightening the futures of those around them harbored no thoughts of the impossible. In them, thoughts of the impossible are supplanted by "I have an idea…" "Just imagine…" and "What if…"

Every happy and successful person, by whatever metric you wish to gauge these, has faced doubt, hardship, failure, struggle, ridicule, and fear—all of them. I submit none of them ever brought into their designs for happiness and success the words, "I can't," or, "That's impossible."

I can, I believe, I can imagine, and That's possible are all open-ended, potential realities without limits. They are infinite in scope. They begin as words in someone's mind, mere thoughts, thoughts which will later become translated into action because new horizons are being envisioned, sweeping vistas sight unseen. Such thoughts will not be held back. They are too powerful.

It is time to choose for you a life without self-imposed limitations. I want you to come to despise the orderly and unyielding flow of variations in sameness the words "I can't" and "That's impossible" seem to impose.

Negative Beliefs

Make a list of five negative beliefs, objections, or notions you have in your head and you feel are preventing you from taking the steps necessary to obtain your preferred future.

Negative Belief #1:

_____

_____

Negative Belief #2:

_____

_____

Negative Belief #3:

_____

_____

Negative Belief #4:

_____

_____

Negative Belief #5:

_____

_____

Now, I want you to make a list of possible solutions for each negative belief. If you have trouble getting started, try to think of what you would say to a friend, someone you really wanted to help, who came to you for help with the same problem. If you get stuck on any one of them, ask for help from a positive, solution-oriented thinker. This could be a trusted friend, colleague, advisor, personal physician, therapist, or a coach like myself.

Solutions to Negative Belief #1:

_____

_____

Solutions to Negative Belief #2:

_____

_____

Solutions to Negative Belief #3:

_____

_____

Solutions to Negative Belief #4:

_____

_____

Solutions to Negative Belief #5:

_____

_____

All negative beliefs regarding change should be approached in this manner. The big loud voice inside your head saying "HECK NO" will never go away, but it can be diminished.

"When it becomes more difficult to suffer than to change... you will change."
~ Robert Anthony

Implement

Implement the plans you have made with a timetable of actionable steps with built-in accountability.

Six Steps Toward Permanent Change

#1. Make a decision. Nothing will change for you until you decide it will change. Figuratively speaking, if you don't like the scenery, you can change the view. If you want some things to change, you're going to have to change some things. You must decide to decide things are going to be different.

#2. Begin now. You are at the starting line of the rest of your life, so start moving. You might not know exactly where the finish line is just yet, but at least you will be moving forward.

#3. Help yourself first. Acknowledge your particular situation. Completely and honestly probe the depth and breadth of it. Know that you can be the agent of change in your own life. Stop waiting for outside forces to give you something, rescue you, or provide for you. Help yourself first. Come to depend on yourself and your own actions for your own needs.

#4. Ask for help if needed. I don't mean a friendly ear to bend or someone that will be content to offer words of encouragement. I mean people, agencies, facilities, providers, institutions, programs, and groups that will offer assistance with your particular issues. This is not in disregard of the third step above. Asking for help if you honestly need help **is** helping yourself. You may need advice. You may need protection. You may need counseling. You may need treatment. You may need a coach. Ask for what you need.

#5. Never turn back. I have seen people extract themselves from deplorable situations only to crawl right back to them in moments of weakness or self-doubt. Protect your weak spots. Develop strategies to protect yourself from the allure of old habits, codependency traps, and situations that have harmed you. Your preferred future always lies ahead of you, never behind you.

#6. Trust in change. You must come to realize that you are capable of more, that you can be different, and create, and learn, and produce, and build, and grow. We grow by how we change. We all have different natural talents and abilities that will compel us to change if we choose to use them. If you're not changing, you're not growing.

These steps are just the beginning, to get you moving so you can begin to embrace the possibilities of change leading to the probability of success. They are intended to stop you from waiting for your future to just happen to you and to put you in control of it instead.

If you are ready to take charge of your future, then I want you to go back to pages 125 - 131 and fill in some dates for each of the action items you have listed. Below is an example of one of the action templates.

Over to the right of Current Circumstance is a small blank space. Using your red pen, enter a firm date on which you will begin moving through your Next Steps for the action item listed. Over to the right of Desired Outcome there is another small blank space. Enter a reasonable target completion date by which time you will have completed the Next Steps and attained your Desired Outcome.

Professional Life
Current Circumstance:

_____

_____

_____

Begin By Date:

_____

Next Steps:

Desired Outcome:

Target Completion Date:

By entering a Begin By date, you are making a COMMITMENT to begin on that date. The completion date is an estimate. It's okay if you don't obtain the desired outcome by the exact date you have entered, but you must try your best if it is a reasonable time frame.

Accountability

One way to ensure you are moving through your action items and steps is to have an accountability partner. This should be someone you trust who you will report to periodically or who will check on your progress. This should be someone positive, optimistic, and motivated, someone who will both encourage and challenge you.

If you don't know anyone like this, then you need a new circle of influencers. If I'm coaching you, it would be me. Your accountability partner could also be a friend, colleague, or advisor, someone other than a family member. This is too much of a responsibility to give someone who might have difficulty pressing you or being detached enough to be objective when necessary.

Make a list of possible accountability partners in order of preference right now and the exact date by which you will attempt to engage them for this important role. It's okay to have more than one accountability partner but no more than two. Use your red pen.

Potential Accountability Partners

_____

_____

_____

_____

Date to Attempt to Engage

_____

_____

_____

_____

It is a good idea to take the sheet(s) with your most important action items and post them where you can see them every day. Post them on your bathroom mirror, your refrigerator, the dashboard of your car, beside your computer at work (the places where you don't mind making them public).

Read over them every day. Keep moving through your Next Steps, always asking yourself, "What's the next step?" which will move you toward our goal. Make adjustment as needed as you go. Cross them off as you go so you can visibly see your progress.

First of all, you will be amazed just how much of your preferred future becomes reality when you write down your goals and begin to take clearly defined steps toward them. Secondly, you will be astonished as to how quickly you begin to reach them.

Transformation

Transformation is acknowledging and documenting your progression from feeling burned out to a new freedom and a new happiness.

As I mentioned before, the first step of transformation is not a physical one. It is a mental step. It requires a change of one's mindset, a transformation in one's thinking. Win, lose, or draw, it is where your hardest battles are fought—in the mind.

> *"Transformation isn't about improving,*
> *it's about re-thinking."*
> ~ **Malcolm Gladwell**

The Difference Between Transformation and Change

Although change and transformation are different sides of the same coin, they are as different as night and day. You can change your hairstyle, your clothes, your car, where you live, your job, and your friends, but none of that will change you, the real you.

Transformation isn't about becoming somebody different either. It is about becoming the more authentic version of you, living a life which is in complete alignment with your core being, fully utilizing all of your unique natural talents and abilities. It is a metamorphosis.

Transformation is not a one-off event. It is a mindset, a new way of living that is intentional and continuous.

Transformational change means fully elaborating your true self and acting accordingly. It is less about taking on a new persona and more about projecting your true persona to the world. You may need to TRANS-FORM before you can **REIGNITE**.

If you have been crossing off your Next Steps and action items as you have completed them, then you have seen the progress you have made, which is important. Monitoring your progress will boost confidence in your ability to adapt and change; rev up your idea, innovation, and creativity engines; open up a new universe of possibilities; and keep you on track as you march toward your preferred future.

There is another important benefit to TRANSFORMATION I haven't discussed up until now. Yet it may be one of the most important reasons for you to transform, or for anyone to transform for that matter.

This reason, should you decide to fulfill it, will become part of your legacy. I have no doubt it will help you to answer the question, "Why am I here?" if you are curious to know. It is for this reason:

"Transformed people transform people."
~ Richard Rohr

I have always imagined I am here in this world, this big old universe, for a reason. You may have thought this too. Most people do.

I have come to feel I'm not here just to serve myself. I have long felt my purpose here is to help others on their journey in life, to pass along the best parts of myself and the best lessons I have learned, to help those who struggle and leave my corner of the world enhanced somehow by my being here. Ultimately, it is in this way we serve ourselves.

I will tell you this, and it is undeniably true. You can never be your best at helping others and you can never live a life of passionate purpose if you are burned out.

What is true passion without purpose? What is true purpose without passion? The combined fires of passion and purpose will never burn out, or burn you out, as long as they are conjoined.

To live a life of purpose with passion, to be fully engaged, demonstrating vigor, dedication, and absorption while using all of your unique set of natural talents and abilities, you must be **ON FIRE** for what you do. When you are, you will know firsthand exactly what I mean when I talk about a new freedom and a new happiness.

If you have **reviewed** your current circumstances, **envisioned** your preferred future, embraced **introspection, generated** ideas and action plans to transform your life, **neutralized** obstacles, and barriers, and **implemented** your plans with a timetable and accountability, then you are already undergoing a **transformation** and are well on your way to **engagement**. You are ready to catch fire and **REIGNITE** if you haven't done so already.

Engagement

Engagement celebrates a purpose-driven work life characterized by vigor (energy), dedication (involvement), and absorption (efficacy) while experiencing a more authentic and joyous life overall. You will notice those three terms are the exact opposite, the antithesis, of the three keyword hallmarks of burnout—exhaustion, cynicism, and inefficacy.

Engagement is your goal. Not just for the immediate future, but for the rest of your life. Not just for your professional life, but for your personal and family life, as well, in all four life realms—mental, emotional, physical, and spiritual.

Engagement signifies a life in balance. A balanced life distills down your life realms and your unique set of natural talents and abilities to form a potent and powerful crystalline version of you, allowing you to reach your fullest potential.

To be engaged in all aspects of living is to become, as my publisher Jesse Krieger so eloquently describes, a fully realized version of you. This becomes the source of immense satisfaction as you live your life to the fullest.

If the state opposite of burnout, **ENGAGEMENT**, is characterized by: **vigor, dedication,** and **absorption**, then the pathways to engagement can also be defined. There are six, and they are the exact opposite of the six major job mismatches that cause JRB.

Six Pathways Lead to Engagement

According to burnout investigator and author Christina Maslach, the six pathways leading to **ENGAGEMENT** are:

- Sustainable workload
- Feelings of choice and control
- Recognition or reward
- A sense of community
- Fairness, respect, and justice

- Meaningful and valued work

Are any of these missing from your workplace? If so, circle in red the ones above which you feel are missing.

These can only be achieved if harmony is created between the employees and their employers in a way which lead to changes in the job environment as well as the workforce. Dr. Maslach has demonstrated very convincingly that burnout or engagement are foremost a function of the job situation and not the individual employee.

This is because individual employees cannot for long carry the total burden of adjusting to fit their job or work environment. At some point, the job must begin to conform to the employee in a way that is conducive to engagement.

Focusing only on the employees who are burning out without a critical look at the work environment is counterproductive due to the economic law of diminishing returns.

This law states if one contribution (the employee's) in the production of a good or service (healthcare, for instance) is continuously increased and all other inputs are held fixed, a point will be reached at which additional contributions (work) by the employee will yield progressively smaller or even diminished results. This is where we are today in my profession of medicine.

When this occurs, employees will either become burned out or be well on their way to burnout. To increase production at this point, one would have to change the entire work environment by making adjustments to every aspect of the production process. Some large organizations are beginning to see this. Most are woefully behind.

This gets us back to the attributes which will define a healthy and engaged workforce—a sustainable workload, feelings of individual choice and control, recognition of reward, a sense of community, fairness/respect/justice, and meaningful/valued work. For large and highly-entrenched groups or organizations, the process of building engagement may be difficult, but it is not impossible. I would say to the individual who loves their job but cannot abide their current work environment that you can become the agent of change in your workplace.

As an initial step, I would suggest opening a dialogue with an administrator in your organization, whether it is a hospital or large provider group. They will rightly want to know what's in it for them. The approach that seems to be most useful is a discussion concerning resources, and by resources I mean money.

The costs associated with JRB in toxic work environments can be devastatingly high. The benefits of fostering engagement in the workplace will add income to the bottom line and are therefore income generating.

Your discussion might also include a list of the major employee-job mismatches from pages 32-46 you feel are present in your current work environment, contributing to your burnout. These, along with the missing pathways to engagement from pages 145-146, will give you a firm footing for a persuasive argument in favor of addressing JRB in your organization.

I've prepared an Executive Summary on JRB. This will be a useful tool for beginning a discussion with your employer or employee administrator on the advantages of eliminating JRB from your workplace and the benefits of nurturing workplace engagement. To download your FREE copy now of the Job-related Burnout EXECUTIVE SUMMARY, go to http://ReigniteBook.com/job-related-burn-out-executive-summary/

"You must be the change you wish to see in the world."
~ Mahatma Gandhi

If you are burning out or completely burned out in your current work environment, it is incumbent on you to be the agent of your own change.

Either you must change or your work environment must change. Tough decisions and choices lie ahead.

If after hearing your concerns your employer is unwilling to change and adjust the work environment, you may need to seek employment elsewhere in order to find a workplace more closely aligned with your core values and preferred future.

The alternative is to remain stuck in an environment where you can neither blossom nor thrive, a work environment you have come to despise.

Moreover, it is a work environment which has called into question your thoughtful decision to enter your chosen profession for serving others.

I hope you will agree with me, working burned out is no way to live this one life.

What is your favorite, inspiring, motivational quote? This would be a good place to write it down to serve as a reminder of your commitment to REIGNITE.

_____

_____

_____

_____

_____

If you're going it alone and these steps have proved to be too daunting for you, then individual coaching is definitely a viable option. I coach burned-out professionals and would be happy to speak with you about your specific needs. If you're interested in being coached, please don't hesitate to contact me through my website at ClarkGaither.com or DrBurnout.com.

RESILIENCE-HARDINESS-WELLNESS

When Resilience Really Counts

have had to deliver a lot of bad news to patients during my practice career. I've told hundreds of patients that they have tumors or cancer, that their spouse has died, that their sibling has died, or that their child has died.

I have had to directly inform patients that they were dying, providing them an opportunity to tidy things up before the end of the precious few days they have remaining. They have no time to waste.

Once, a little girl was solemnly brought to my office by her mother. She pulled me aside and asked me to inform her daughter that her father had been killed earlier that day in an automobile accident. She just couldn't bear to deliver the horrible news herself. Everyone will face tragedy or crisis in their life at some point. This is a requisite symptom of the human condition. Since everyone is unique, everyone will handle a crisis in their own way, but some common themes will emerge.

When bad news is delivered, some people will stare at the floor or their hands and go silent, trying to weigh the precise meaning of the words I just uttered and how they will be affected by them as they seem to settle into a kind of benign resignation.

Some people will glower at me, blinking, but emotionless at first, as they begin to question the accuracy and validity of the news. They will reach a state of denial rather quickly. It is the quintessential defense mechanism on full display.

Others will become more animated and begin to ask questions ever more rapidly, sometimes even before I can fully answer the last one. They are rushing headlong into the future with their bad news in tow in hopes of learning something that will change the course of their destiny.

A few will immediately and dramatically decompensate with completely uninhibited and loud weeping, wailing, and bemoaning. Good or bad, it becomes a spectacle for all to witness.

Oddly, some will actually look relieved, even smile, because in a strange way their worst fears have been confirmed, their morbid prognostications verified, their inner convictions validated. They are happy that they were right. They are vindicated.

Panic will cross the face of many as the full impact of the unhappy and unwelcome news is felt. Almost everyone sheds tears before they leave the office. I always have a box of tissues handy for them, and sometimes for me.

Not so long ago, I had to tell a patient that her breast biopsy was positive for cancer. She became tearful, but her overall look was one of resolve. She had no intention of throwing in the towel. She squared her shoulders, faced me directly, and asked appropriate questions. She wanted to know exactly what she needed to do in order to ensure her chances of survival. I could tell that she was determined to survive, and that is always a great sign of a more positive outcome.

I have noticed that when faced with the possibility of death, very few people will actually give up completely. Whether for themselves or for their loved ones, most will fight for survival, fiercely in fact. That is called resilience.

I have often thought that I want to be that resilient if and when my time comes, like the last example of the lady with breast cancer. Yet when I look back on my own life, I can see where I have given up over choices and situations that were much less threatening to me. I didn't fight.

Many bad and undesirable things have happened to me over the course of my life, just as they have to you, dear reader. Most were because of the choices I made, others because of the actions of others I could not control.

There were so many times I acted, or failed to act, out of fear because resilience was outside of my comfort zone. I often chose the path of least resilience. As a result, I reacted to crisis and tragedy in almost every one of the non-resilient ways I have just described.

I made a decision some time ago to try and face every challenge with resilience. I have not always been successful. Old habits are sometimes hard to break.

When I have chosen the path of resilience in the face of crisis or tragedy, difficult situations always improve more quickly, more possibilities for surviving and thriving emerge, recovery is more complete, and lessons are always learned, leaving me better off than before.

I have learned when resilience really counts—always.

Do you feel you are resilient? How do you handle a crisis or tragedy?

Ten Steps Promoting Resilience You Absolutely Must Learn

Resilience is such a great word. The word holds so much sparkling promise to me. We use the word resilience in psychology to describe the ability of people to bounce back from adversity. It is a trait common to people who, when knocked down by life, simply spring back with renewed and dedicated intent to overcome hardship and come back even stronger than before. It may be the ultimate key to happiness and wellbeing.

Resilience is marked by such characteristics as optimism, positive attitudes, the ability to regulate and attenuate emotions, and an enduring capability to see failure as an opportunity to learn and grow. Following misfortune, the resilient among us are able change course, marshal their inner strength, and soldier on.

Resilience is often missing from people who are either burned out or burning out in their work, relationships, or living. Resilience is a key factor in fostering engagement through purposeful work. Engagement, with the three hallmarks of vigor (energy), dedication (involvement), and absorption (efficacy), is the exact opposite of burnout.

Resilience isn't something only a few people can have. It is a compilation of thoughts, behaviors, and actions. Anyone who is not resilient can become resilient. It is a learned behavior. But like any acquired skill, it must be practiced.

So, how does one attain resilience? What steps can be taken?

Here are ten steps which will promote resilience:

- Successive approximations toward your goals. Break large projects into smaller more manageable bits and move through them sequentially. This will lessen the impact of mistakes along the way.

- Be decisive. Indecision is the playground of doubt. Weigh the available options, then decide. Accept no wiffle-waffle in yourself. Project no indecision toward others. You won't always make the correct decision being decisive or by being indecisive. Being decisive saves valuable time.

- Avoid catastrophizing. Don't view problems, mistakes, and failures as insurmountable. They never are, and I can prove it. If you don't surmount them, someone else will.

- Maintain a high-altitude perspective. Always keep an eye on the big picture to avoid drowning in the minutia.

- Connect with like minds. Nothing fosters perseverance more than hanging out with positive people who persevere.

- Greet change with flexibility and adaptability. Change is inevitable. Change is necessary. It is the only way to get from bad to good and from good to better, even if you have to go in the opposite direction sometimes to get there.

- Capitalize on failure. Failure will teach you what you did wrong or what you need to know if you remain open to learning. Consider this: no one else may know what you may have learned from your failures. That is valuable information.

- Be optimistic. It costs no more in mental energy to think optimistically, and you'll feel a whole lot better versus pessimistic thinking. Plus, you'll generate more solutions and great ideas with optimistic thinking versus pessimistic thinking.

- Acknowledge your feelings. It's okay to feel emotional pain from anger, loss, or sadness. Feelings are neither good nor bad, they just are. Whether good or bad depends on what you do with them. Just realize you don't have to live with them 24/7 and you don't have to let them prevent you from reaching your goals. Look forward to feeling better, and time will take you there.

- Be whole. Attend to your mental, emotional, physical, and spiritual needs. You cannot be resilient with a life out of balance.

Practice these steps daily, and over time resilience will become your default position for handling problems, stress, adversity, and tragedy. Resilience can make the difference between a life well lived, one with passion and purpose, or a life steeped in misery, lost in bitterness and regret.

Are you resilient? Can you bend in the winds of change without breaking? Can you bounce back from adversity and tragedy? There are many things a person can do to develop or strengthen resilience.

Nine Ways to Build or Strengthen Resilience

One aspect of being transformed means having the quality of resilience, which simply means possessing the ability to recover from adversity. Lacking resilience can leave people stuck, paralyzed to the point of being unable to move forward. Everyone should have this trait because the consequences of lacking resilience can rob you of a brighter future.

Difficulty, tragedy, hardship, and suffering will come to everyone in one form or another if you live long enough. That is just living life on life's terms. We might not have a choice in the bad stuff that may come our way in life, but we do have a choice in how we respond.

Being able to adapt, cope, adjust, confront, carry on, endure, survive, move on, or move forward—these are all qualities of resilience. I see too many people who lack resilience get stuck. They suffer the same tragedy or the same trauma over and over again. They stop growing. They stop enjoying life. They stop trying to better themselves. It doesn't have to be that way.

There are several steps you can take in order to become resilient or to strengthen resilience. Just know that what works for one may not work for all and no strategy will work right away. As with any skill, learning to be resilient takes time, practice, and patience. But this is very doable for anyone with a desire to transform into a better way of living.

1. **Build self-awareness.** Stay in touch with how you feel. Suppressing negative emotions is not adequately dealing with them. People often avoid painful feelings because, well, they're painful. But, when you feel ready, it is best to face emotional pain head on in order to move on. If negative emotions aren't dealt with adequately, they will just keep reappearing and leave you stuck.

2. **Hold on to the big picture.** Whatever happens, try to put things in perspective. How many times has something bad happened to you in your past and you thought, "My life is over?" Yet more often than not, those unwanted episodes in your life turned out to be the best thing for you at the time. You just didn't realize it then.

3. **Let time be your friend.** I had a terrible tragedy happen to me a little over five years ago. It was worse than bad. It was mind-numbing and shockingly devastating, but I knew that I wasn't going to feel that way forever. Just knowing that offered some relief. It would have been easy to continue to wallow in self-indulgent pity, but there is just no future in that, and I knew it. Time does heal all wounds, if we allow it to happen. Allow time and perspective to work their magic for you.

4. **Get moving.** I tell this to patients every day. Your legs are connected to your brain. If your legs are moving you forward, that means your brain is moving forward. Whenever you exercise, there are neurotransmitters that are released like dopamine, endorphins, enkephalin, epinephrine, and others. These make your brain feel good, which will make you feel better. They help relieve anxiety and depression. Exercise works as well as our best medicines for treating mood disorders.

5. **Learn acceptance.** You may as well. You can choose to deny what is happening or what has happened to you, but that will not allow you to live in Realville. Acceptance is giving yourself permission to

move forward. Acceptance will be a bitter pill to swallow at times, but just like any medicine, it may be bitter at first but then you get better.

6. **Set goals and move toward them.** I believe this is one huge factor in letting go of tragedy. Setting goals and moving toward them requires forward motion. Early on, this provides the distraction the brain needs in order to move forward. In the fullness of time, attaining goals that were set during tragedy provides the context necessary for closure. This has worked in my own life.

7. **Be optimistic; avoid negativity.** It's easy to talk down when you are down. Talking up will lift you up, even if just a small amount. When things seem to be crashing in on you, be as positive as you can be and reach out to the positive and uplifting people in your life. They will help hold you up, even when you don't feel like standing. You are as you think.

8. **Have a strong social network.** I don't know what I would have done were it not for family, friends, and colleagues when my life seemed to implode. Having a strong social network makes all the difference in being resilient. Also, as you draw strength from others you will be in a better position to one day return the favor to those you know are in need.

9. **Be kind to yourself.** No, you aren't perfect. No one is, so allow it for yourself. If you're feeling broken, become whole again by taking care of your four realms—the mental, emotional, physical, and spiritual—along with the healing power of time.

These are just some of the many ways to build and strengthen resilience. Add anything else that has worked for you in the past.

Do you feel that you are resilient? How has resilience helped you to weather life's storms?

Nothing Out of the Ordinary

The successful entrepreneur, the methamphetamine addict, the renowned artist, the active alcoholic, the stay-at-home spouse, the thief, the politician, the murderer, the physician, the gambler, the baker, the hooker. All of these individuals have something fundamental in common. I believe without exception they are, each and every one, extraordinary.

We all start out the same—naked, afraid, and helpless. All of us began our journey with a unique set of natural talents and abilities. We were born possessing different ways of looking at the same things. We describe and feel different things differently. In this regard, we are also all the same—unique.

There are no ordinary people. There will never be another exact copy of any one of us ever again on planet earth, or in the entire universe for that matter. The odds of you being you have been estimated to be 400 trillion to one. By the way, 1 trillion seconds=31,709.70 years.

We are powerful, precious, and potent potential personified.

So, are we all extraordinary, luminous beings, spectacular in nature, capable of wondrous things at any time during our brief existence? Or are we just as apt to lead unpremeditated, boring, mediocre, inconsequential lives with little or no meaning? What determines this?

Is it destiny, or circumstance, or luck, or birthright, or cruel irony that determines the life we will lead? For relatively few, these may hold sway. I believe for the vast majority, they do not.

As I said, there are no ordinary people. Why then do so many extraordinary people live ordinary, inconsequential lives or even tragic, self-degraded existences? The answer is deceptively simple: too many extraordinary people making too many ordinary choices.

Too many stop searching. Too many say, "I can't." Too many say, "It's too hard." Too many feel, "I don't deserve this." Too many sit down when they should stand up. Too many resign when they should fight. Too many walk when they should run. All of these extraordinary people making ordinary choices.

The extraordinary, ordinary choosers look at the successful, passionate, happy, fulfilled, resilient, and serene people and think, "How lucky they must be," when in reality, it is purely a case of extraordinary people making extraordinary choices for themselves and those they care about.

It could be so for everyone. But it won't be. Too many of the extraordinary will be content with ordinary choices in life. Too many more will be discontent but will still choose to maintain the status quo.

Only a relative few will seek a different path. They will create, explore, build, write, and innovate. They will scintillate with passion for a purpose. They are the ones, the extraordinary ones, who have made extraordinary choices. They see nothing out of the ordinary.

There are no ordinary lives, only ordinary choices.

Do you believe you are extraordinary? If not, why not? Or, do you feel you are extraordinary but living an ordinary life of your own choosing? If so, what are you going to do about it?

YOUR FOUR LIFE REALMS

Ten Reasons Why Only 2% Will Transform

I am talking about the percentage of people in any patient population that will radically change their lifestyle in ways necessary to profoundly alter and improve their health. It is 2%.

The percentage of people who are willing to completely TRANS-FORM their entire life into something that is more meaningful and purposeful to them is about the same, 2% or less. A very famous and successful self-help speaker once lamented that 70 percent of those who buy his products will never use them, and those are the people motivated at least well enough to attend his seminars.

Why? What are the reasons for this? You are probably familiar with many of these ten reasons, although there may be a few you haven't considered:

- **Fear.** Fear of failure mostly. I believe this to be the largest impediment to personal progress. There is no obstacle that anyone can place in front of you larger or more imposing than that of self-generated fear.
- **Procrastination.** This is a form of anxiety over starting or completing a task, especially new or difficult tasks. Ironically, procrastination creates more stress in the end than it alleviates.

- **Lack of Focus and Clarity.** These twin attributes are crucial to beginning a transformative change. They supply us with orderly direction, a list of current needs, and a defined audience to serve.
- **Lack of self-awareness.** Having self-awareness helps define priorities, provide an understanding of an individual's current status, and identify areas where change is most needed in order to progress forward. Lacking this leaves you stuck.
- **Improper planning.** Setting goals is absolutely imperative, both little ones and big ones, short-term and long-term. Most often, people will stall out of the gate because they fail to build in some easier wins that can be obtained in the short run, which provides needed momentum.
- **Lack of personal responsibility.** Individuals who look to blame others, including God, for their lack of success or look to others, including God, to provide them with personal success will be forever stuck in Nowhereville.
- **Avoiding accountability.** Accountability keeps us motivated, honest, and moving forward toward our goals. Avoiding accountability is a form of self-sabotage.
- **Lazy.** Defined as an aversion or disinclination to work; indolent. As a practicing physician I can tell you with absolute certitude that there is no pill to fix laziness. But this has never stopped some people from asking me for one.
- **Progress is not measured, acknowledged, or celebrated.** All of these need attention. Are you moving forward? Yes? How do you know if you don't measure for progress or have a means for measuring progress? Also, it is not enough just to know from whence you came. Periodically assessing how far you have come provides valuable context. No points are subtracted from success if you dance in the end zone a bit after a win. I think we are supposed to feel good about success. Don't you?
- **Conventional Inertia.** I coined this term as a substitute for "same ol,' same ol,'" or "stuck in a rut," descriptions of merely existing

rather than living. This is the realm of the comfortably miserable, a state of intentional, low- expectation stagnation. This condition is perceived as a lower risk environment in which to be but in actuality it carries the highest risk of all. Upwards of 98% of the population suffers from this condition.

Most people want to be part of the 2%, but 98% will never work this list in any actionable way. Breaking free of conventional inertia and overcoming the rest of these barriers is certainly possible. People do it every day. What it requires is broad-scale, TRANSFORMATIONAL thinking and action, a change in mindset.

If you are in the 2% who have transformed your life already, you know this to be true. You have pursued your passions and overcome these barriers one-by-one. You have discovered happiness through the purposeful work of your choosing. You have stood in defiance of fear and conventional inertia and have redefined your life using your natural talents and abilities.

If you are in the 2% group, which of these barriers were most difficult for you to overcome? Are there others?

If instead you feel you are in the 98% group, the question you have to ask yourself is: which of these barriers to transformation are holding you back? What actions will you take today to transform your life and join the 2%?

ORGANIZATIONAL REMEDIES FOR JRB

This chapter is written for employers who would like to eliminate the causes of burnout from their organization or for employees who would like to stay with their company but would like to know how to go about transforming their work environment into something better.

More often than not, the employee becomes the focus of efforts to alleviate the symptoms of burnout in the workplace by attempting to teach them stress-reduction strategies. This can be very demeaning to an employee, to haul them into a room for a series of lectures or workshops on stress reduction. The subtle message becomes, "You are too stupid, inept, or ignorant. You just don't know how to properly handle your own stress, so we are going to teach you how."

If there is any message which should be repeated often and loudly, each and every time the topic of employee burnout comes up for discussion, it should be this:

Employees do not burn themselves out.
It is usually the work environment that
burns out the employee.

The Cure

Programs and training designed to detect and mitigate any job- employee mismatches causing burnout or to prevent job-related burnout in the first place through:

- Instruction
- Workshops
- Measuring
- Programs to eliminate, mitigate, and prevent employee burnout
- Monitoring
- Ongoing management

Learning to recognize job-related burnout when it appears in the workplace, along with identification and mitigation of the underlying causes, can improve employee satisfaction, prevent high employee turnover rates, decrease customer complaints, and improve customer satisfaction. This has the potential to both save and generate large amounts of capital.

Look for the first signs of job-related burnout—rising employee dissatisfaction, high employee turnover rates, and decreasing customer satisfaction. If job-related burnout in your workplace is suspected, a burnout checklist can be applied to gauge the depth of the problem. Alternatively, a workplace consultation or assessment for burnout conditions could be obtained.

It begins by assessing the workplace for the presence or degree of burnout amongst the employees. This might include the application of the MBI, Maslach Burnout Inventory. It is the industry gold standard for measuring the extent of burnout amongst employees in the workplace.

The MBI directly measures the level of emotional exhaustion, depersonalization, and the lack of a sense of personal accomplishment where present. These are the three hallmarks of job burnout. The MBI will assess for these with a high degree of sensitivity and specificity. This also provides a mechanism for measuring the outcomes of any interventions.

The next step would be to determine the presence and degree of the six major job mismatches between the employee and the job that will cause employees to burn out. Just to refresh, these mismatches are: work over-load, lack of control, insufficient reward, breakdown of community, absence of fairness, and conflicting values.

A workplace survey is used to look for the presence of these six major mismatches. The Areas of Worklife Survey, by Christina Maslach and Michael P. Leiter, should be the workplace survey of choice. It is thoroughly explained in their book, *The Truth About Burnout*. This survey measures those six areas of the work environment which are the most relevant to employee's relationships with their work: Workload, Control, Reward, Community, Fairness, and Values.

Once the underlying causes are known, mitigation and prevention strategies can then be designed and deployed. Follow up becomes the third and last component of a full workplace consultation for job-related burnout. For prevention, vigilance through ongoing, periodic reassessment becomes fundamental.

If the conditions for job-related burnout are found to be present, much can be done to mitigate or ameliorate its effects. In addition to eliminating mismatches from the workplace, resilience training can prove useful.

Resilience is the state opposite of burnout. Resilience is characterized by vigor, dedication, absorption—what every administrator wants in every employee within their organization. These results are more than cost effective and are transformational.

The Bottom Line

High employee turnover is often caused by job-related burnout. The detection, mitigation, and prevention of job-related burnout is an extremely cost-effective solution. An assessment and intervention for job-related burnout, coupled with resilience training, could be the "make or break" difference for any organization with high employee turnover.

So, how do you get an organization that is burning out its employees to spend money on programs to identify and eliminate burnout form the workplace? How do you get cost-conscious administrators to invest in these initiatives?

You must speak in terms they understand and can identify with completely. You must talk money. You must make a compelling case for change by showing them how much employee turnover is costing the organization and how much money can be saved by programs and workplace redesign to eliminate burnout causing job mismatches.

Eliminating or preventing job-related burnout isn't just cost effective, it's income generating. Here's how:

- Decrease employee turnover and improve retention of needed talent
- Increase employee satisfaction and decrease employee complaints
- Decrease employee absenteeism
- Decrease workplace injuries
- Improve customer satisfaction and decrease customer complaints
- Increase the quality of products and services
- Eliminate workplace hostility and promote workplace harmony
- Decrease the threat of lawsuits

This is a process, an educational one, and it can take some time. The only alternative is to continue working in a miserable and toxic work environment. This begs the question, "What if there is absolutely no interest in changing the work environment where I'm currently employed?"

This is a hard position to be in but one in which millions of people find themselves in every day. More times than not, the best decision for yourself is the most difficult one to make. If all things remain the same, burnout doesn't improve. It gets worse with time.

Change is healthy; change is good. Be the agent of change at your workplace; change jobs; change yourself. Just change.

What to Expect from a Consultant
Leading Employees from Job-related Burnout to Engagement
The overarching goal for hiring a consultant is to reduce burnout and foster engagement in the workplace. The following steps are fairly typical

of what a consultant might suggest or employ when consulting for an organization with suspected high employee burnout rates.

Step 1. Overview—interview the consultee concerning current workplace problems/issues, identify and summarize clear-cut goals, prioritize intervening efforts, and sketch out an actionable timeline.

Step 2. Apply the Maslach Burnout Inventory (MBI) to every individual in the targeted employee group(s).

The Maslach Burnout Inventory, developed by Christina Maslach and colleagues, is the industry gold standard for measuring the degree of job burnout in individual employees. It takes about ten minutes to complete and can be performed online. This instrument has excellent sensitivity and specificity and is an invaluable metric for gauging the effectiveness of burnout elimination strategies.

Step 3. Hold an MBI results briefing.

The consultee is briefed on the implications and ramifications of aggregate MBI results. Comparisons with similar, normalized groups can be made. The results are shared in aggregate with those who participated in the survey.

Step 4. Apply the Maslach Areas of Worklife Survey (MAWS) to targeted employee group(s). The Areas of Worklife Survey:

- Is a short questionnaire.
- Identifies key areas of strengths and weaknesses in an organizational setting.
- Has demonstrable reliability and validity across a variety of occupational settings.
- Measures relevant mismatches between the work environment and employee that can cause burnout or matches that lead to engagement.
- The relevant areas targeted are Workload, Control, Reward, Community, Fairness, and Values.

Step 5. Hold a MAWS results briefing.

The consultee is briefed on the implications and ramifications of the MAWS results. Comparisons with similar, normalized groups can be made. The results will clarify and focus efforts on reducing and eliminating workplace job-employee mismatches that cause burnout while enhancing matches which foster engagement.

Step 6. Apply the DISC personality profile to targeted employee group(s) and administration.

Individual communication styles can be vastly different based on personality. This will greatly affect how people communicate, or fail to communicate, effectively in the workplace.

Understanding individual communications styles is key to improving communication, which ultimately enhances the work environment. The DISC personality profile helps people to understand their own behavioral style, how to recognize the other styles, and tailor their behavior accordingly.

The four personality styles are Dominant, Influential, Steady, and Conscientious.

Step 7. Hold a DISC introduction and briefing.

Employees receive an overview of the DISC personality profile in a group setting. This includes a brief history of the profile, a discussion of its validity and usefulness, and a full description of the four personality styles.

Each employee receives a one-on-one discussion of their individual profile results and how to make the best use of them when communicating with individuals of the other personality styles.

Step 8. Design workplace interventions and programs to mitigate, eliminate, and prevent the major identifiable causes of job-related burnout and to foster engagement in the workplace.

Step 9. Assist with implementation of interventions and put a plan in place to track progress.

Step 10. After a predesignated period of time, resurvey targeted employee group(s) with the MBI and MAWS to gauge the effectiveness of workplace interventions.

Step 11. Hold a post-intervention survey briefing with the consultee. Adjust current intervention strategies or design and implement new ones if needed.

This is just an example of how a consultant might engage with an organization for the purpose of identifying, mitigating, eliminating, and preventing workplace burnout. Steps can be added, modified, or eliminated. The consulting experience should be specifically tailored to the unique needs of the organization and its employees for the most effective benefit.

The Other Option: Self-Employment—Entrepreneurship

If you find those in control of your current workplace environment have no interest in improving, then they have no interest in you. Or, if you have experienced burnout multiple times in the same or different industries, at this point I would refer you back to the chapters on Individual Remedies for Job-Related Burnout. This would signal the time to punch up the resume, begin a new job hunt, or seriously entertain the notion of starting that business of your own you've been thinking about.

If a new job, your dream job, is what you're after, I highly recommend the book *48 Days to the Work You Love* by Dan Miller. This book contains proven pathways to meaningful and purposeful work that is more closely aligned with your talents, abilities, core values, and personal goals.

If you are thinking of an entrepreneurial pursuit with an eye on lifestyle, then I would definitely read *Lifestyle Entrepreneur* by Jesse Krieger. Find an entrepreneur, and you will find optimism; that's where the energy, innovation, and creativity lie. I think we should surround ourselves with entrepreneurs.

Better yet, I think everyone should become an entrepreneur, whether as your vocation or avocation.

Take a look at just some of the statistics, facts, and figures about entrepreneurship compiled in a most excellent infographic by Nicole Schlemmer as featured in *Entrepreneur,* entitled *46 Facts You Should Know About Entrepreneurship.*

- One in 18 people on the planet own their own business.
- The average age of an entrepreneur is 40.
- Less than 1% come from either extremely rich or extremely poor backgrounds.
- There are no developed countries represented in the top 25 most entrepreneurial countries.
- The US ranks only 42nd as the most entrepreneurial country.
- Two out of three people think being an entrepreneur is a good career choice.
- 75.4% have worked at other companies for more than six years.
- 70% of entrepreneurs are married.
- 95.1% of entrepreneurs have bachelor's degrees.
- The entrepreneur is three times more likely to have rebelled as a teenager.
- 21% of graduates started a business because of unemployment.
- The number of women entrepreneurs increased 30% from 2007-2012.
- The USA is the #1 country for female entrepreneurs.

If you haven't started this noble quest of continual self-improvement and self-discovery called entrepreneurship, what are you waiting on? Who are you waiting on?

The only one that needs to show up is you! The quest will provide you with everything else you need.

But you must begin.

The world is now open for business. With a laptop or smartphone and an internet connection, you have the entire planet at your fingertips. Whatever you do, don't continue to labor along at a job you detest feeling miserable and burned out. Don't you owe it to yourself to explore what else you can do to make a difference in your life and the lives of others?

ENGAGEMENT—THE POLAR OPPOSITE OF BURNOUT

You are now very familiar with the three hallmarks of burnout: emotional exhaustion, depersonalization, and a lack of a sense of personal accomplishment. The salient keyword features of the burnout syndrome's three dimensions are exhaustion, cynicism, and inefficacy.

To be burned out means to be completely miserable in your work. People who suffer from burnout dread Mondays, they long for the weekends or for more time off, and hate what they do throughout the workday, which never seems to end.

But what is the opposite of burnout, and how is that defined? The positive antithesis of burnout can be described in a single word—engagement. To be engaged is to be completely present in your work. In fact, work is no longer viewed as work when one is fully engaged. No longer considered labor, work becomes a wellspring of joy and pleasure through intentional and purposeful effort to create or produce using one's unique set of natural talents and abilities.

An onlooker would be hard pressed to tell if a fully engaged individual is actually working or playing. That's because a fully engaged individual does not work. They are simply expressing who they are by what they do. They are demonstrating to the world their passion and purpose.

Creativity and innovation are unbridled in the engaged individual. Ideas, optimism, and positive thoughts flow from a person who is fully engaged, like water from a natural spring.

An expert may work and say, "Look at what I can do." Someone who is burned out will work and say, "Look what I have to do." Someone who is engaged and has found their purpose in life and is pursuing it with passion will shout, "Look at what I get to do!"

Engagement has the salient features of energy, involvement and efficacy, the exact opposites of exhaustion, cynicism, and inefficacy. It describes a positive job-related state of mind characterized by:

- **Vigor**—high energy, mental resilience, a willingness to invest effort in one's work, and persistence in the face of difficulties. Keyword: ENERGY
- **Dedication**—a strong involvement in one's work with a sense of significance, enthusiasm, inspiration, pride, challenge, and achievement. Keyword: INVOLVEMENT
- **Absorption**—happily engrossed and so concentrated in one's work that time passes quickly to a point where one has difficulty separating and detaching from work. Keyword: EFFICACY

Wow! Do you feel that way about your work? If you do, you are fully engaged. If not, well, maybe the time has come for some introspection followed by intentional actions to change your circumstances.

VIGOR

If you are burned out at work, the chances are you feel a lack of energy and drive. In fact, the only drive you may have is just to survive the workday, or to hold on until the weekend. The lack of emotional energy in job-related burnout often translates to physical exhaustion as well. Can you relate?

Have you seen people who genuinely enjoy their work and seem to have all the energy in the world for their job? If this is how you feel about your job, then that's awesome. You've probably found your true passion and are fulfilling your purpose in life.

You are in the zone. You don't feel at all like you are laboring or slaving away at your work. Instead, you feel light and energetic as you make steady progress toward completing tasks. You are producing more than ever before and you feel 100 percent engaged. If you had to describe this in one word it might be vigor.

Vigor is an inner drive, a feeling of active strength with a healthy sense of mental and physical power. When you have vigor, you feel completely vital and you approach work activity with an energetic intensity or force.

Vigor is the first hallmark of work engagement. Individuals who are engaged will:

- Report positive emotions
- Enjoy robust health
- Report feelings of job happiness and satisfaction
- Create their own work experience and find their own resources
- Chare the attributes of engagement with others

For perhaps 90 percent of workers, vigor is something that is diminished or absent when it comes to their job. In fact, vigor is usually the first attribute that is lost when suffering from job-related burnout.

If you are wondering if you lack vigor when it comes to your work life, ask yourself this question: Do you seem to lack adequate energy to do your job properly yet find more than enough energy to do whatever you want once you are away from work?

If the answer is yes, you probably do lack vigor. The question then becomes: Do you lack the other attributes of engagement—dedication and absorption—as well? If so, you have burned out at work.

If you are burned out, there is a 90 percent chance it is not your fault. There are six major mismatches between the job and the employee that lead to burnout. You can take an on-fire, dedicated, purpose-driven employee and place them in the wrong work environment, and they will burn out every time. It doesn't have to be this way.

Vigor, dedication, and absorption, the essence of work-life engagement, can be fostered where absent and enriched where present. It begins by identifying the job-employee mismatches and then eliminating them from the workplace.

Do you feel you lack vigor? Do you feel you have demonstrated this first hallmark of job-related burnout?

DEDICATION

Ask any boss about hard-working, key employees who drive their businesses forward, and one of the words they will invariably use to describe them is dedicated. Dedication is an exceedingly strong feeling of support and loyalty for something or someone. To run any successful enterprise, you must have available, dependable, dedicated employees.

Dedication is the second attribute or hallmark of worker engagement, the first being vigor. Engaged employees are what every employer wants. Feeling engaged at work is what every employee wants. To feel engaged while on-the-job is to love one's work.

On-fire, purpose-driven, dedicated employees are often the first to show up and the last to leave work. Sometimes, they have to be reminded to quit working and go home, to take a break or eat. It is hard for them to break away; they love what they do so much.

This isn't because they are workaholics or toil long hours out of fear of losing their jobs. They genuinely love what they do. At the beginning of every work day, they are anxious to get started.

They feel energized by what they do. They feel they are making a difference. On some fundamental level, they **are** the difference. Have you ever felt this way about your work?

Here are nine unmistakable signs of employee dedication:
- A visible, almost infectious passion for one's work
- Positive attitude and demeanor in personal interactions with other employees and with the patients, clients, or customers
- Punctuality at all times for work, meetings, and functions
- High attendance/low absenteeism at work, meetings, and functions.
- Knows the history, mission, values, and vision of the business
- Demonstrates initiative often
- Flexibility when it comes to change

- High work ethic
- Reputation for getting things done

The opposite of worker dedication is worker cynicism.

A business burning out its employees will never thrive. Employees who are burned out will eventually leave their workplace when the pain of staying becomes greater than the pain of leaving, of making a job or career change.

Burned-out employees are easy to spot. They are not dedicated. They are miserable. They may be present, but most of their day is spent begrudgingly doing just what they are required to do and no more, biding time until they are away from work. They long for the weekends and dread Mondays. Have you recognized this in others? Have you ever felt this way about your work?

The good news is an absence of dedication doesn't have to be permanent. If you no longer feel dedication toward your work, perhaps it is time to ask some basic questions. If you have an unhappy workforce with high turnover, perhaps it is time to determine which of the major job-employee mismatches are burning out your staff and provide needed remedies.

Do you feel you are burning out or already burned out? Is your work in alignment with your core values? Are you doing your life's work, what you were called to do, using your own natural and unique set of talents and abilities? Do you love what you do but hate your current workplace environment?

Answering these and other questions can give you some direction and clarity as you choose the right next steps. It is possible to find purposeful work for which you are passionate and dedicated. If you own a business, it's possible to create a work environment which fosters an engaged and dedicated workforce.

ABSORPTION

Everyone knows someone who is a workaholic. Perhaps that someone is you. Workaholics work extremely hard They work long hours. They work and work and work to the exclusion of nearly all else in their life.

What, then, is the difference between someone who is a bona fide workaholic and someone who is simply but tenaciously absorbed by what they do? If either one is healthy, which one? Can both be bad for you?

Work absorption is the third attribute or hallmark of work engagement. It is characterized by efficacy, a feeling opposite of inefficacy or the lack of a sense of personal accomplishment.

Workers totally absorbed by their work are what every employer wants. For the sake of work enjoyment, feeling absorbed by one's work is what every employee wants.

If you are absorbed by your work, you are completely immersed in what you do. You love what you do. You can't wait to do what you do. You are constantly and proudly telling other people, "Look at what I get to do!"

You are demonstrating to the world who you are by what you do because a large part of what you do is who you are.

While looking at someone who is completely absorbed by their work, it often becomes difficult to decide if they are working or if they are playing. When fully engaged in work a completely absorbed worker may have to be reminded to take a break, to eat, or that it is time to go home. They have found happiness and contentment on one main avenue of their life—meaningful work. More than likely, a truly absorbed individual is fully utilizing their unique set of natural talents and abilities to the fullest. They have become a fully realized version of themselves.

Workaholics, on the other hand, tend to feel driven in some way to do what they do. It is a matter of compulsion, not enjoyment. They may or may not feel happy with their work. In fact, dissatisfaction seems to run high and they can often be heard complaining about, how much work they "have to do."

Here are some of the major differences between an individual who feels absorbed by what they do and a workaholic:

ABSORBED	WORKAHOLIC
Generally happy with work.	Generally dissatisfied with work.
Feels pulled in by work.	Feels pushed toward work.
Intrinsically motivated.	Interpersonally motivated.
Feels compelled to work, but freely.	Works compulsively.
Often oblivious to the time.	Races against the clock.
Works hard because it's fun.	Works hard, even when it's not fun.
Works precisely and effectively.	Works excessively and ineffectively.
Fully engaged in work.	Can easily suffer burnout.
Most likely their life is in balance.	Likely their life is out of balance.

Both the absorbed worker and the workaholic have difficulty disengaging from work. However, the motivations underpinning the difficulty in disengaging are much different. The absorbed worker has difficulty because work is so much fun. The workaholic has difficulty because the underlying motivation is a compulsion to work, not enjoyment.

It should now be crystal clear, being and feeling absorbed is a happier and healthier state in which to work than workaholism. There is one caveat, though. Anything which is good for you can become bad for you in excess.

People who are fully engaged in their work, as reflected by vigor, dedication, and absorption, can become workaholics if they are not careful. All work and no outside play will make Jack or Jane eventually hate their jobs, even if work seems like play. A well- rounded life rolls along with the least effort.

The key is to strike a balance between one's work life, family life, and social life, taking care to not let one become overriding causing another to suffer. All four realms—mental, emotional, physical, and spiritual—want and need attention. Each supports the other. Let one suffer, and all will suffer.

Even if you feel completely absorbed in your work, take the time to enjoy all of what life has to offer. Never work until you feel it is all done or like you must do it all now. Leave something at work undone for tomorrow. Leave some room for creative, innovative, possibility thinking. Create a little tension, a sense of anticipation for what comes next.

In so doing, there will never be any real dread about returning to work. With an almost tranquil anxiousness you will look forward to getting back to the work you love, feeling blessed you have it to do.

Do you feel absorbed by your work, or are you more of a workaholic? Are you doing your life's work, what you were called to do, using your own natural and unique set of talents and abilities? If you feel you are more of a workaholic, have you considered making some changes to this one life you've been given?

It is possible to find purposeful work for which you are passionate, to feel truly engaged as exemplified by vigor, dedication, and absorption.

Remembering the Six Pathways to Engagement

You now know the hallmarks or symptoms of job burnout—emotional exhaustion (exhaustion), depersonalization (cynicism), and a lack of a sense of personal accomplishment (inefficacy). You also know the six job mismatches that can cause a person to burnout—work overload, lack of control, insufficient reward, breakdown of community, absence of fairness, and conflicting values.

I have just identified for you the state opposite of burnout, which is ENGAGEMENT characterized by vigor, dedication, and absorption. The pathways to engagement can now be defined. There are six, and they are the exact opposite of the mismatches which cause burnout.

According to burnout investigator and author Christina Maslach, the six pathways leading to ENGAGEMENT are:

1. Sustainable workload
2. Feelings of choice and control

3. Recognition or reward
4. A sense of community
5. Fairness, respect, and justice
6. Meaningful and valued work

These can only be achieved if harmony is created between the employees and their jobs in a way that leads to changing the job environment as well as the people. Dr. Maslach has demonstrated very convincingly that burnout and engagement are foremost a function of the job situation and not the individual employee.

This is because individual employees cannot carry the total burden of adjusting to fit their jobs. At some point, the job must begin to conform to the employee in a way that is conducive to engagement.

Focusing on just the employees who are burning out without a critical look at the work environment is counterproductive due to the economic law of diminishing returns.

Introduced earlier in the book, this law states if one contribution (the employee's) in the production of a good or service (healthcare, for instance) is continuously increased and all other inputs are held fixed, a point will be reached at which additional contributions (work) by the employee will yield progressively smaller or even diminished results.

When this occurs, employees will either be burned out or well on their way to burnout. To increase production at this point, one would have to change the entire work environment by making adjustments to every aspect of the production process.

This gets us back to the attributes which will define a healthy and engaged workforce—a sustainable workload, feelings of individual choice and control, recognition of reward, a sense of community, fairness/respect/justice, and meaningful/valued work. For large and highly entrenched groups or organizations, the process of building engagement may be difficult, but it is not impossible. I would say to the individual who loves their job but cannot abide their current work environment that you can become the agent of change in your workplace.

A single individual can have an enormous impact, not only on the mechanics of their work situation but the philosophy and culture of their work environment as a whole.

In the meantime, do you feel more burned out or engaged? Do you see any of the six mismatches between you and your work at your current job?

FROM BURNED OUT TO ON FIRE

Happiness In the Pursuit of Dissatisfaction

want you to be dissatisfied, dissatisfied with your work, your play, your free time, your relationships, your goals, your hopes, and your dreams. In short, I want you to be dissatisfied with your entire life as you are currently living it.

Before you ask, "What's wrong with you?" hear me out. I think the word dissatisfaction has gotten too much bad press. Are you completely, supremely satisfied with every aspect of your life? Are there things you would change?

If the answer to the second question is no, it means you are quite pleased with the status quo. You are satisfied with everything. You are in attitudinal equilibrium with everything and everyone around you. You are beyond even a petty annoyance. Your life is complete. You are content. You are serene. There is no desire to improve anything, nor is there any hope to improve anything.

This is complacency, and it sounds like death by boredom to me. If I am not growing and stretching, it means I am stagnant. I would rather assume room temperature than reach a state where I no longer want to advance in this life, to learn a new skill, take on a new role, innovate, or create something new.

If there are things you would change about yourself or your life, then by definition you are dissatisfied with them. I think dissatisfaction is the greatest motivation for change, perhaps the only one. Without dissatisfaction there would be no great artists, musicians, engineers, writers, businesses, CEOs, or entrepreneurs, only poor to mediocre ones. Do you think Henry Ford, Ernest Hemingway, Steve Jobs, Richard Branson, or Yo-Yo Ma were, or are, ever satisfied?

Here are seven truths about dissatisfaction, Gaither's Axioms of Dissatisfaction, if you will.

- **Supreme dissatisfaction is the only path to excellence.** It is an absolute requirement. If you are completely satisfied with the way things are, you have become part of the status quo.
- **The status quo will lead to obsolescence, always.** Dissatisfaction will hasten the arrival of the obsolete. Satisfaction will ensure it. To become obsolete, just stay the same. The world will pass you by without noticing.
- **All progress is the product of change carried out by people who are dissatisfied.** Leaders are never satisfied. That is why they are leaders. The satisfied follow them.
- **The degree of your dissatisfaction=the degree to which you will change.** The more unsatisfied you become with a task, a product, a relationship, a cause, or a career, the more energy you will pump into changing things for the better and the more dramatic the results will be.
- **A willingness to change, although required, is not necessarily a motivation for change.** A mere willingness to change is a reflection of insufficient or acceptable dissatisfaction. You must become dissatisfied enough to compel yourself to change some things if you want some things to change.
- **Dissatisfaction without action is resignation.** Chronic complainers who boldly state what is wrong and what should be done but do nothing have resigned. They have ceded their power to someone or something else.

- **You can be at once both happy and dissatisfied.** Supreme happiness comes from continually pushing on your limitations and tearing them down. You do this because you are dissatisfied. Happiness is in the pursuit of dissatisfaction.

Life is short. Begin to actively and aggressively chase your dreams. Shun the status quo. Tear loose the bonds of self-limiting behavior. Throw down the barriers you've placed on your own path. My last hope for you, dear reader, is a day of complete and utter happiness in the pursuit of dissatisfaction.

Successfully Avoiding Burnout (Slow and Steady!)

Highly motivated and energetic individuals often fail to reach their goals or bring a project to a successful conclusion because they burn out or run out of steam before the project is completed. Has this ever happened to you? It has happened to me countless times. You come up with a great idea, a fantastic idea. You throw a loose plan together and begin to spend time and resource on it at a frenetic pace. You hit some snags, but you keep grinding away.

Problems arise, but you lay them aside because you want to bring the project to a conclusion quickly. As difficulties mount, they begin to have a real impact on your efforts, which require more and more of your time and attention.

Your efforts begin to stall. You become discouraged. What seemed like a thrilling venture turns into a laborious task that you now seem to avoid. Once again, you feel like a failure.

I can't tell you how many times this has happened to me in the past. It is something I guard against, but I let this happen to me again just recently. I was out for a run, training for a 10K race, and my plan was to run six miles in a certain amount of time. It was already hot and humid. I started out way too fast, but at first, I thought, "this isn't so bad." Even though I knew I should slow down, I didn't listen to my gut instinct.

I blew up and had to walk some after four miles and then again at five miles. I never finished the six miles I had planned to run, turning in only 5.5, and I was way over the time limit I had set. I had just wanted to get it done, but in my haste I failed to complete what I had set out to do.

A worthy task, goal, project, creative work, or life is not a race. If you view them as such, you will probably lose out every time because in those instances, you are only racing against yourself.

If there is something that you wish to do that is worthy of your time, effort, and resources, then slow and steady work is how to get things completed. You want to position yourself for successive approximations toward your goals. In other words, in progressive steps.

Do you have a specific project in mind? Here are 7 ways to help you shepherd that idea to completion:

- Develop a full plan or outline. Take the time to do this. It will save you time later. This is your map or guide to get you from point A to point B. Without one, you will be lost.

- Set a realistic timeline. Spread your energy and enthusiasm out over time. If you don't spread these out, you will burn out.

- Break large projects up into smaller segments. No one sits down and writes a novel from beginning to end in one session. It is usually written in one to five-page segments daily. Checklists help with this.

- Slow and steady progress beats sprinting out of the gate. Marshal your energy and efforts so that you can go the required distance and finish.

- Don't look to others to gauge your own progress. Keep your eyes on the task (road) in front of you. You can't watch where you are going if you are distracted by what others might be doing.

- Aim for small victories. They are like water stations along a race route. They refresh, reinvigorate, and propel you forward. Get rid of the all at once-or-nothing mentality. It is self-defeating. Celebrate the small success. If there is a setback along the way, adjust and move on.

- Enjoy the process. If you know where you are headed and are determined, you can relax. Don't become so unidirectional and engrossed that you can't enjoy the creative experience, which is enjoyable in and of itself. Then, you will come to know the full joy of your creation the moment you deliver it to the world.

Can you identify with burning out on a project before it is completed? What steps can you take, or have you taken, to avoid this scenario?

IT'S ALL UP TO YOU!

Whether you have burned yourself out because your life is out of balance or whether you have burned out due to a toxic work environment, I hope there is one message which came through loud and clear from this book. It doesn't have to be this way. If you recognize someone who is burning out or burned out, please reach out to them, and share this message with them too.

Either you can change or you can change your circumstances. Don't just sit and smolder.

REIGNITE!

NEED AN INSPIRING SPEAKER FOR YOUR NEXT EVENT, ORGANIZATION, OR GROUP?

Dr. Clark Gaither, best-selling author of *Reignite* and *Powerful Words*, will make your next event the best one yet!

SPEAKING TOPICS:
- Professional Job-Related Burnout—How to identify, mitigate, eliminate, and prevent worker burnout.
- Wellness: What It Is and What It Is Not
- Work-Life Balance
- The Dramatic Differences Between Stress and Burnout

Go to ClarkGaither.com/contact for more information
or to book me as a speaker for your event today!

REIGNITE

Framework at a Glance

~Transformation from burned out to ON FIRE! ~

Review—your current circumstances and the events that have led to them.

Envision—your brightest preferred future.

Introspection—take an inventory of your core values and honestly assess the condition of all four of your life realms—mental, emotional, physical, and spiritual.

Generate—a plan of action to transform your life.

Neutralize—all of the self-placed obstacles and barriers.

Implement—the plans you have made with a timetable of actionable steps with built in accountability.

Transformation—acknowledging and documenting your progression from feeling burned out to a new freedom and a new happiness.

Engagement—celebrates a purpose-driven work life characterized by vigor, dedication, and absorption while experiencing a more authentic and joyous life overall.

REFERENCES

American Foundation for Suicide Prevention. *10 Facts About Physician Suicide and Mental Health.* https://www.acgme.org/ Portals/0/PDFs/ ten%20facts%20about%20physician%20suicide. pdf.

Centor RM; Morrow RW; Poses; et. al. *Doc Burnout—Worse Than Other Workers.'* Medscape. 2012 Nov.

Inui T; Safran DG; et al. *Doctor Discontent: A Comparison of Physician Satisfaction in Different Delivery System Settings, 1986 and 1997.* Journal of General Internal Medicine. 2001 July; 16(7):452-459.

Kaiser Family Foundation. *National Survey of Physicians—Part III: Doctors' Opinions about their Profession.* 2002 March. https:// kaiserfamilyfoundation.files.wordpress.com/2013/01/highlights- and-chart-pack-2.pdf.

Maslach C; Jackson SE. *The Measurement of Experienced Burnout.* Journal of Organized Behavior. 1981; 2:99-113. Doi:10.1002/ job.4030020205.

Maslach, C; Leiter MP. *The Truth About Burnout: How Organizations Cause Personal Stress and What to do About it.* San Francisco: Jossey-Bass. 1997. http://psycnet.apa.org/record/1997-36453-000.

McMurray JE; Linzer M; Konrad TR; Douglas J; Shugerman R; Nelson K. *The Work Lives of Women Physicians Results From the Physician Work Life Study.* The SGIM Career Satisfaction Study Group. Journal of General Internal Medicine. 2000 Jun; 15(6):372-380.

Peckham C. *Medscape Lifestyle Report 2016: Bias and Burnout.* 2016 Jan 13. https://www.medscape.com/slideshow/ lifestyle-2016-overview-6007335.

Pololi LH; Krupat E; Civian JT; Ash AS; Brennan RT. *Why Are a Quarter of Faculty Considering Leaving Academic Medicine? A Study of Their Perceptions of Institutional Culture and Intentions to Leave at 26 Representative U.S. Medical Schools.* Acad Med. 2012 Jul; 87(7):859-69. https://www. HopkinsMedicine.org/women_science_medicine/_pdfs/Why_Are_a_ Quarter_of_Faculty_ Considering_Leaving.2012%20onlineproof.pdf.

Shanafelt TD; Boone S; Tan L; et al. *Burnout and Satisfaction With Work-Life Balance Among US Physicians Relative to the General US Population.* Arch Intern Med. 2012 August; 172(18):1377-1385. http://archinte. jamanetwork.com/article.aspx?articleid=1351351.

Shanafelt TD; Hasan O; Dyrbye LN; et al. *Changes in Burnout and Satisfaction With Work-Life Balance in Physicians and the General US Working Population Between 2011 and 2014.* Mayo Clinic Proceedings. 2015 Dec; 90(12):1600-1613. http://dx.doi. org/10.1016/j.mayocp.2015.08.023.

The Physicians Foundation. *A Survey of America's Physicians: Practice Patterns and Perspectives.* 2012 Sept. http://www. physiciansfoundation.org/uploads/ default/Physicians_ Foundation_2012_Biennial_Survey.pdf.

VITAL Work-Life & Cejka Search. *Physician Stress and Burnout Survey.* 2011 Nov. https://cdn2.hubspot.net/hubfs/471821/Client_ Materials-

Documents-Flyers-Handouts/VITAL_Worklife_ Cejka_Survey_
Report_and_Addendum_02.15.pdf. .

A free ebook edition is available with the purchase of this book.

To claim your free ebook edition:

1. Visit MorganJamesBOGO.com
2. Sign your name CLEARLY in the space
3. Complete the form and submit a photo of the entire copyright page
4. You or your friend can download the ebook to your preferred device

Morgan James BOGO™

A **FREE** ebook edition is available for you or a friend with the purchase of this print book.

CLEARLY SIGN YOUR NAME ABOVE

Instructions to claim your free ebook edition:
1. Visit MorganJamesBOGO.com
2. Sign your name CLEARLY in the space above
3. Complete the form and submit a photo of this entire page
4. You or your friend can download the ebook to your preferred device

Print & Digital Together Forever.

Snap a photo

Free ebook

Read anywhere